Interior Alchemy

S-T
G-H
U-V
THE ROYAL NATURAL HISTORY

INTERIOR ALCHEMY

Secrets to Creating Expressive Ambience

REBECCA PURCELL

WITH KATHY WALTON

PHOTOGRAPHS BY STEVE GROSS AND SUE DALEY

William Morrow and Company, Inc.
New York

Library of Congress Cataloging-in-Publication Data

Purcell, Rebecca.
Interior alchemy : secrets to creating expressive ambience /
Rebecca Purcell.
p. cm.
Includes index.
ISBN 0-688-14894-8
1. Interior decoration. I. Title.
NK2110.P87 1998
747—dc21 97-34689
CIP

Printed in the United States of America

First Edition

1 2 3 4 5 6 7 8 9 10

BOOK DESIGN BY JENKINS & PAGE (NYC)

www.williammorrow.com

This book is dedicated to:

My Dad who, perhaps without knowing it, taught me style and allowed me to be anything I wanted.

My Mom who inspired me to be everything I wanted.

The Waldorf School, which opened the world to me.

[A c k n o w l e d g m e n t s]

Grateful acknowledgment to the following people for their inspiration and help:

Kathy Walton

Amy and Chris Clavelli

Jeffrey Jenkins

J. Morgan Puett and Mark Dion

Bryan Purcell

Sir Richard Dayne

Loren Pak

Ann Foxley

Paulette and Evan Cole

Elyse Cheney

Kathleen Hackett

Gail Kinn

[Contents]

Interior Alchemy

[How to "Hoosh" an Interior]

In a sense, this is an antidecorating book. Creating a home is a discovery process, not a matter of ornamentation or setting the right things in the right places. It's about creating a living space that feels right and therefore looks smashing. When you express your internal predilections externally, you can evoke a moving and dynamic environment. *Interior Alchemy* is about pursuing what pleases you in making a home and making your pleasures all fit together. Express your passions, display what turns you on, find out what makes you feel comfortable and connected, and there you will find the perfect home. With a few simple secrets to help you along, this book is designed to help you find your way to the living space that is truly your own.

The homes in these pages all belong to people who have built their environments around their own quirky passions and points of view. What each of them shares is a love for old things—for flea market treasures as well as real antiques. What drives most collectors and flea market addicts is a love for things with the taint of life on them.

Vintage pieces, antiques, found objects, all bear the visible signs of history. It may be a set of deliberately carved initials in a child's desk, some mysterious notes scribbled in the margins of a book, or simply a crude repair. What we call "patina" is no more than the accidental accumulation of such marks: worn spots, natural darkening, scratches and scars on the surfaces of things. All are the signature of decades or more of human use, and they conjure up images about lives lived before us.

One of the magical aspects of shopping for the things we love, the "gotta-have-its," is the scavenger hunt effect. When you hit on some fabulous piece that's been hiding out in a junk store or flea market, it's like discovering a buried treasure. Now I'm not talking about getting a great Tiffany lamp for only $1,500. I'm talking about getting a crazy, hideous 1970s lamp for $3, changing the shade, and making it look great. People who have already caught the bug know what I mean—it's a big high! It's all about personal vision and creativity—creating something out of nothing, transforming the ugly into the beautiful, or simply turning the not-quite-it into the just-right. Think sow's ears into silk purses. Think Rumpelstiltskin, spinning straw into gold.

My own collecting habits began when I was a small child. I loved to save objects from nature and things other people had discarded. I collected stones, shells, tiny plastic charms, china animals, colorful leaves—each time feeling certain that I had saved something precious from a life of obscurity. I was a scavenger.

I transformed my childhood passions into my adult profession when I became a retail display artist. While creating displays for Macy's in Atlanta, I learned perhaps the most important decorating skill I've ever known. I want to share it with you; it's the secret formula in *Interior Alchemy*. From my earliest mentors, a crew of local display artists with a no-holds-barred sense of style that liberated me, I learned how to "hoosh."

Hoosh was a localism that meant display. As in:

"The top of that armoire needs a good hoosh."

"That table looks great, it just needs a little more hooshing."

"Heavens, it's already ten o'clock. I have to get hooshed."

"Hoosh that cabinet."

A hoosh is an arrangement that works, that has a sense of balance and its own internal coherence. At home, this means taking disparate objects and furnishings that you have and making something whole out of it, something with weight and presence. Hooshing also involves transforming things: finding great collectibles and turning out cunning fakes with staining and aging techniques and some Do-It-Yourself art.

But the most important thing you will need to add to the things you already own may be a fresh outlook—rethinking the placement of your furniture and decorative pieces, and having the courage to experiment. You can hoosh everything from a collection of vases, bottles, books, boxes, fabrics, dolls, toys, and brushes, twigs, or bones . . . anything that turns you on. You can hoosh furniture so that the pieces speak to each other. You can hoosh an entire room so that it has a nice feeling of movement from space to space. You can hoosh walls by filling them with pictures all the way up to the ceiling. And you can hoosh a room by understanding how to work with its horizontal and vertical planes—of walls and floors—by connecting them in mindful, interesting ways. The real art of hooshing lies in coming up with solutions to design problems using the materials at hand.

Each chapter in this book displays a different fabulously hooshed house or apartment. Some spaces are large while others are small; one is really tiny, showing how problems of different orders become the mothers of some very interesting inventions. There's the Attic-style space bursting with collectibles that give the sense of having been layered over time. The Spare home has a Zenlike spatial quietness, and clearly makes the most of the visual planes. The Alienated apartment has a kind of future Gothic feel, a place where Victorian meets *Blade Runner* with absolutely original results. The keys to each style are offered in each chapter, which points out the fundamentals that get you the right effects. And there are step-by-step, illustrated instructions for some Do-It-Yourself projects, including original picture matting and framing. You can even hoosh up your own chandelier! That will get you going.

The ideas in *Interior Alchemy* may inspire you to take chances and play with your furniture. You've already got everything it takes—just make yourself at home.

[One: **Attic**]

Pages 4–5
Not all hooshes need to be full! An old fan, a birdcage, a shell—the items on this dresser are poetic enough to stand on their own. This is a good example of what to do when you have enough full hooshes but do not want to leave a large surface, like this dresser, bare. Note that the painting creates a backdrop so the items can be loose but there is still a feeling of "fullness."

If your favorite weekend activity is cruising tag sales and flea markets, Attic may be your element. Attic is for the no-holds-barred collector—the kind whose tastes run from eclectic to omnivorous. With Attic, less is not more. And more is always possible.

The range of collectibles in the Attic-inspired home of Amy and Chris Clavelli spans the end of the 19th century through the 1940s, decades when our great-grandparents saw half a century of entrenched Victorian style make way for the engines of the machine age. Think of the anarchy and energy of the Roaring Twenties—an era when the sleek new Philco radio in the parlor was probably topped by an embroidered dresser scarf and a faux Ming vase. All those form-follows-function dictates of the Modernists produced lots of streamlined appliances and furniture through the 1920s, 1930s, and 1940s, but at the same time the markets were flooded with exuberant, mass-produced kitsch that blissfully ignored every rule in the book: porcelain figures from Japan, Kewpie dolls, beaded fringe, skyscrapers built to look like hood ornaments . . .

The Clavelli home has that sort of vitality, with its cheeky mix of objects ranging from turn-of-the-century charmers to early modernism, from whimsical tchotchkes and carnival souvenirs to heirloom-quality pieces and serious art. What pulls it all together is the sort of subtle organization that suggests layers that have accumulated over time. Layer upon layer of evocative clutter, like great-grandmother's attic—where the visions and sentiments of one generation have settled in with the one before it, and the one before that.

A painter and collage artist who also works in advertising, Amy Clavelli is one of those collectors who seem to have a sixth sense for uncovering treasures at the flea market: here an Edwardian lamp for $25, there a red Victorian box for $2. Her exuberant approach to collecting is matched by an enviable chutzpah. Once, traveling in a restricted corner of the world, she was determined to get her hands on some underground art. This required a lot of detective work which included covert excursions into the underbelly of the city. Undaunted, she gathered a sizable collection at unbelievable prices, sealed it in her baggage, and ferried it safely past the border guard. Among collectors, she's as intrepid as they get.

Amy's husband Chris, an actor, travels regularly for his work. As astute a collector as Amy, he finds great stuff at small secondhand and junk stores in states like Tennessee, Florida, and Alabama—as well as in upstate New York and Maine. A few of their finds come from stoop sales down the block and little shops on Atlantic Avenue in Brooklyn, where they occupy a one-bedroom apartment in a classic Brooklyn brownstone, complete with a back porch.

Their recently discovered treasures have been added to a collection that started with inherited furnishings and family memorabilia. There is a story behind nearly every piece: whether it's the tiny pink-painted dresser in the bedroom that was found in an antiques shop, or the Greek doll her grandparents brought back from their travels when Amy was small, or the millefiori lamp that belonged to her mother, or the first painted box Chris made for her when they were dating. In many ways this collection mirrors the couple's eight-year-long relationship, and weaves that history together with earlier stories and vintage pieces handed down from each side of the family. The sleek chrome chair in the living room, the sofa from Amy's grandmother, the Art Nouveau clock on the mantel, the classic old Emerson table fan—all meld together in a colorful collage, the sort of fabulously eclectic collection you'd hope to discover in the attic of a house that's been in one family for generations.

Many avid collectors get their start with family keepsakes, hand-me-downs, and heirlooms as diverse as the eccentric uncles and in-laws that populate the family tree. One of the charms of Attic is its air of genteel anarchy. Two sources of influence and inspiration helped to bring that focus to the rooms shown here. One is the owners' passion for the baroque architecture and carnival glitter of the French Quarter in New Orleans. The other is Chris and Amy's equal passion for the art of Florence Stettheimer, whose work includes both flapper-era paintings and beautiful dollhouses—the latter complete with tiny paintings by Picasso and Chagall. In many ways, classic dollhouses have a distinct kinship with Attic: think of the anachronisms, the cunning make-dos, the clear colors faded by time. Stettheimer's work is on display at the Museum of the City of

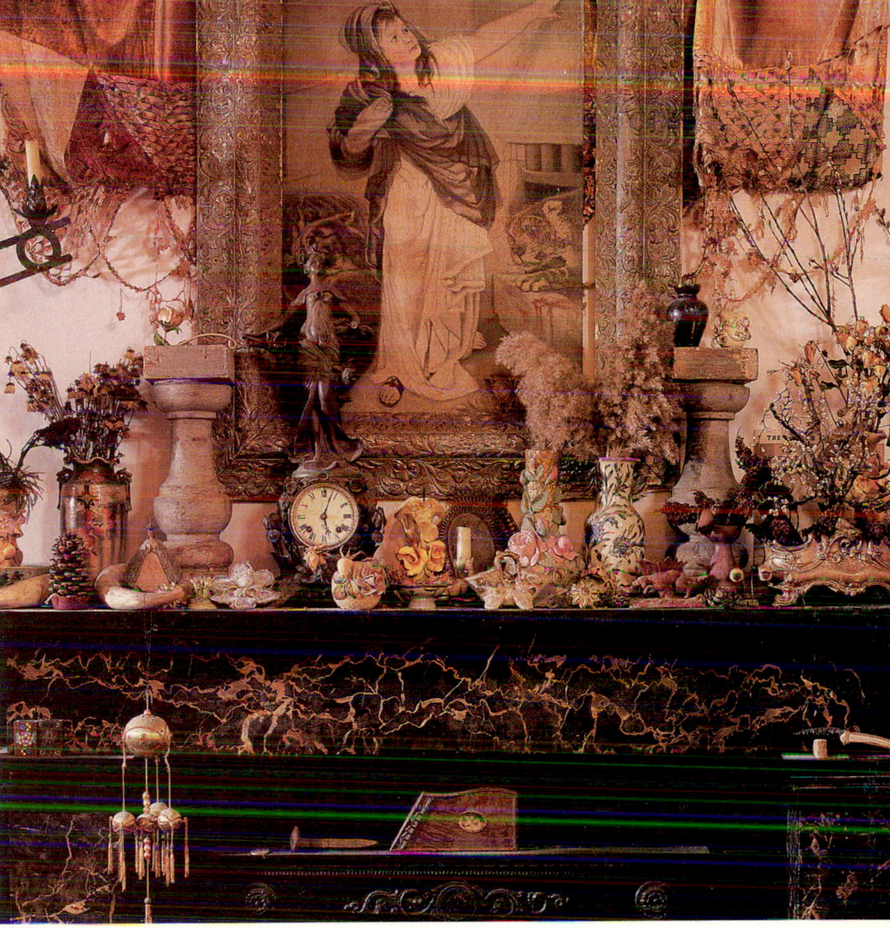

A mantel is the classic area for a hoosh—it is not a utilitarian area, so enjoy filling it up. This particular display is anchored in a triangular composition with the painting as the apex, then the old wooden architectural columns, and graduating down from there.

Abbildung der h. 14 Nothhelfer in Frankenthal.

New York, which houses a fabulous dollhouse collection.

You can energize your Attic scheme—and yourself—by finding your own sources of inspiration in images that stir your imagination. Whether it's a Stettheimer dollhouse, a photograph of your great-aunt's parlor, or an illustration of Toad Hall, any of these is likely to prove more durable than reproduction Victoriana or "English Country" showcases.

Colorful paper lanterns from Japan contrast with framed collages of treasured family photographs. Casually stacked and piled, this corner hoosh is a perfect example of the Attic concept of settled layers. Not all hooshes need to be consciously composed; this one is charming in a way that suggests "it just got that way!"

Keys to Attic

Pile up layers of history. It's the appearance of layers that have accumulated over time that gives Attic its distinctive look. Layer on layer settling in, like drifts of snow over a long winter.

Grandmother is a better guide than Mario Buatta. Avoid the magazines at the checkout counter. Pay attention to those images that haunt your memory. It may be your grandfather's workshop, the Biltmore Hotel, or reading *Wuthering Heights*—historic houses, old book illustrations, and classic movie sets are all potential sources of inspiration.

When you're looking in magazines for ideas for authentic vintage looks and classic interpretations, *World of Interiors* is the best and most beautiful resource. It's expensive as magazines go, but my friends and I collect and cherish every issue. Purchasing it has become a monthly event—sometimes we even buy a bottle of wine as we pore over each page.

Old lace needs a taint of arsenic. Unless it's a vintage specimen, cotton eyelet should stay in the nursery—and if it's obvious Laura Ashley, give it to the little girl next door! A scheme that includes a lot of Victoriana can get saccharine faster than you can say Beatrix Potter.

Take color cues from your older collectibles. Resist sunny prints, bright reproductions, and hues not invented before 1960. On newer fabrics, try the aging techniques described later in this chapter.

Use simple retail display tricks. A few easy design principles can be used to show off treasures and transform your favorite junk into an arresting still life.

A matched pair of bombé chests like these are often seen flanking an entranceway, but putting them together and treating them as one piece can be more interesting than the usual formal arrangement. Here the stacked-and-layered idea is carried out with a tiny pink dresser that straddles both chests. This arrangement breaks the rules in a way that's fun and useful: it's a repetition in miniature (a third dresser), and it forms a triangular composition. Even when they're not doll-sized, furnishings that haven't found a comfortable niche may look great stacked one on top of the other. Surprisingly artful hooshes can result when you're simply trying to save space, especially if you experiment. Don't be afraid to break the rules—the most outlandish combinations may turn out to be inspired.

Relax! One of the big advantages of Attic's domain is that *nothing* is supposed to be pristine. In fact, if you're very fastidious about dust—go to the next chapter.

Use textiles to soften and add color. Whether it's draping diaphanous scarves, fabulous remnants, and swatches over a chair, table, or bed, fabric adds another layer of lived life to the Attic atmosphere. Aging those fabrics takes you one step further into the attic and back in time. Drapery and curtains are essential to the Victorian feel of this style, so bring on the bolts.

Hooshing Small Objects

Like the Clavellis, I love things with a checkered past—things with the taint of life on them. This is the passion that turns many curious and artistically inclined people into flea market junkies. Maybe artist Joseph Cornell's beautiful boxes were an early inspiration for the trend. In the 1930s, he began constructing his strange and evocative assemblages, creating a kind of local history of Manhattan from found objects. In his settings, the everyday domestic castoffs of ordinary citizens become extraordinary talismans. The poet Charles Simic calls his work "dime store alchemy."

It's all too easy, however, for the flea market junkie to wind up with a headache-inducing jumble or with uninspired rows of stuff laid out on every level surface—like a big salad bar. As a style, Attic is eclectic, a hubbub of different eras and elements, but with a subtle, organic sense of organization underpinning it. Sometimes it comes about naturally—like Amy Clavelli's corner hoosh that "just got that way." Sometimes you have to work your own dime store alchemy.

The Pyramid Principle of Display

How do you put all those great little objects into places that will make them shine? Different locations or settings will require different solutions, but one of the most basic and useful organizing principles in display work is the triangle or pyramid formula. Here's an undistinguished spread of objects, your beloved collectibles looking as if they were back

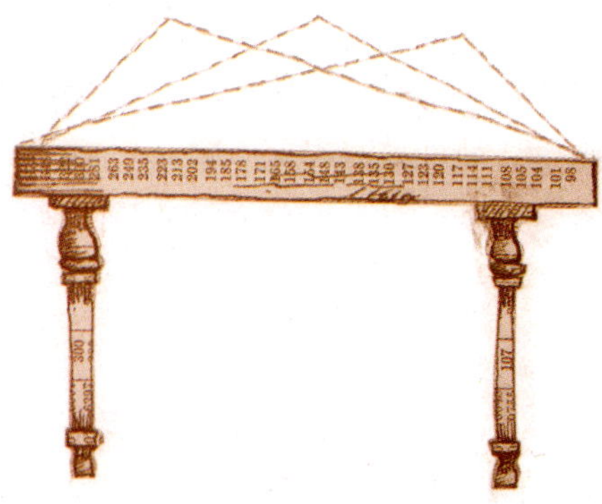

on an outdoor flea market table. Simply rearranged into a triangular composition, they become an effective display. Start by creating height either in the center or, as I prefer, slightly to the right or left of center. Either use your tallest and most massive object at the apex, or stack things together to create a central mass that will visually anchor the display. Then taper out to each side with gradually smaller items. When I do tabletop displays, I start with one large item (a vase, statue, elaborate lamp, small shelf or cupboard) for the central piece, then build out with medium-sized objects, tall, slender pieces (candlesticks, architectural elements), and numerous small bits.

Dotted throughout are pieces that are either soft or soft in form: sachets, antique silk flowers, glass flowers, fruits, shells, dried flowers or greenery. Then I finish it off with a runner or a few yards of old trim, ribbon, or creeping vine to

JESUS SAVES
HEAVEN. WAITS FOR THOSE WHO GET

weave and twist through the collection, binding it together, so to speak. If you have an arrangement that seems to need something, adding one or two of these elements may be all it takes to pull it together.

Display tip 1: Try imagining a history or vignette for arrangements of collected objects: How could this particular assortment have accumulated in this spot? I was once inspired by a pair of old men's shoes: expensive, lovingly cared for, but very well worn. I imagined a gentleman down on his luck, and from that exercise a whole display took shape.

Display tip 2: If items are stackable, stack 'em up. It's a great look for books, boxes, doll furniture, baskets, tins, and textiles.

Display tip 3: Does that 1950s Russel Wright green make the Staffordshire look queasy? However broad and loose it may be, it helps to determine a basic palette for each hoosh.

Display tip 4: If you have a collection of tiny objects, group them. Thimbles, buttons, rocks—try grouping them on an old plate, or pour them into a handsome box. Put the container on a coffee table or somewhere it can be easily browsed through. Or thread individual trinkets on ribbon, thin chain, or wire and suspend them from cupboard and furniture pulls, doorknobs, chandeliers. I've used tiny perfume bottles and earrings on pull chains for lamps and even to decorate a small table.

Display tip 5: Don't be afraid to mix objects from different periods and genres. Think about shape, color, material. Does a wonderfully crusty piece of pottery look merely crude elbowed in with your faceted glass? Remember to add height with tall pieces and include at least one relatively massive element—whether it's a fat vase, a lamp, or a pile of old books.

Display tip 6: Create visual abundance. Unless your collection is already enormous, chances are you're spreading it too thin. Start by choosing a few particular locations to set up displays. Give each "still life" all you've got, and let your collectibles fill one space before they colonize another. Following this rule of thumb can make the difference between clutter and clutter extraordinaire.

Display tip 7: Get vertical with cubbyholes, frames, and shelves. Tabletops tend to be landing strips for bric-a-brac, but don't limit your hooshes to horizontal surfaces. Go up the walls instead—it's a prime way to show off treasures that might otherwise go unnoticed in that third-row lineup across your dresser.

One of my favorite showcases is the sort of wooden cubbyhole that often shows up at the flea market—old hardware bins and the like (not printer's drawers—way passé!). Mounted on the wall or stood on end, these are great for showing off trinkets. A tall bookcase, hutch, or cabinet can also look great filled top to bottom with collectibles—but do *fill it up*. The Attic look especially calls for some dishevelment and jumble, so throw in some old ribbons as well as twigs, flowers, pebbles, eggshells—whatever odd bits strike your fancy—until you've stuffed it full. In Attic, *overstuffed* is good.

Display tip 8: A *shadow box* is a more permanent arrangement and more work—but the end result can have a lot of impact. Take inspiration from Joseph Cornell and mount two, three, or a dozen objects in a deep frame or box with a glass front and either a wood backing or one made of cardboard that's been covered with fabric, a scrap of vintage wallpaper, an old print or photograph, or the like. Set one or more collectibles on the bottom ledge; you can

There's no reason utilitarian storage can't double as effective display, and in fact a kitchen cupboard is a made-to-order frame for a good stacked-and-layered hoosh.

Fabrics draped in unexpected places—on the frame against the wall, for example—and lavished on the bed add a sumptuous touch, as do the gorgeous throw pillows. One or two pillows covered in beautiful fabric will add a distinct sense of opulence to any setting, and they're easily made. The fabric can come from a beautiful old dress or coat, or from a splurge on an expensive fabric—you'll only need a yard or so per pillow.

"float" smaller pieces in the frame by wiring them to the cardboard back. If the box has one or more dividers, all the better. Glue old photos or prints to the back of selected sections, then arrange collectibles on the divider "shelves." Your homemade version may not be as grand as those constructed by Cornell, but you can turn a tableful of clutter into something artful and lovely by arranging the pieces on a vertical plane and putting a frame around them.

Using Textiles to Unify and Soften

Textiles are an all-important element in a scheme that includes a multitude of objects. As a unifying element, a swag or panel of fabric hung on the wall behind an arrangement can be used to balance the palette in that particular hoosh; it will also pull the hoosh together by giving it a visual frame. Experiment to see what colors set off your collectibles best—you can raid the closet or try scraps of colored paper to narrow down the range.

Textiles also add an important element of softness to a room, offsetting all the collectible "hardware" that dominates the Attic decor. Drapes, decorative pillows, cushions, rugs, upholstery—even something as simple as throwing a fringed shawl over the back of a chair—all help to add the comfort and luxury of fabric to a room. Try draping a sash or tying a scarf someplace unexpected, or hang a great dressing gown or piece of vintage clothing where it can be seen. Even if they're too old and fragile to wear, antique clothes and accessories can be used wherever you need to add the softness of fabric. Using clothing as a prop is another trick of the trade in retail display. Take advantage of it at home to add real presence to a hoosh—and show off your vintage *soft*ware.

If you find reasonably priced vintage fabric in quantity—enough for curtains, for example—pounce. Some shops specialize in vintage linens, although many of these run toward early modern prints and may not fit into your scheme. However, I've come across a lot of 1950s dresses at flea markets that are in workable fabrics and patterns, and their voluminous skirts provide ample yardage for pillows, chair cushions, and window valances.

The Alchemy of Aging Fabrics

If there's one element that's consistent in a very eclectic collection, it's aged, patinated color. Antiques and older collectibles need a setting that reflects their muted tones. That includes subtle

color on the walls (more on this in Chapter Six, "Alienated") and aged, subtle color in fabrics and draperies.

Many of the great textiles in the home shown in this chapter are vintage pieces, but some—like the silk organza sheers in the living room—are new fabrics that have been "aged" using a simple ingredient you can find in any grocery store: instant coffee.

I don't really like tea-staining, although you hear a lot about tea-stained fabrics these days. It's usually very pink. It's pretty, but I want my fabrics and papers just to look *old*. Coffee gives a warm, yellowed cast that's a good mimic of real old age. And the instant kind makes it easy to prepare and adjust the exact shading you want, from a faint golden tint to a warm amber brown.

Aging Fabric Using Instant Coffee

Four to five soup spoons of instant coffee in a couple of gallons of warm water will do the trick when what you want is just a subtle yellow wash for a curtain or pillow covers. Double or triple the amount of water and coffee if you're staining a very large piece or thick, heavy fabric. It's easy to test the shade by dipping a corner before you plunge in, but be sure to let the sample dry completely before you decide whether the wash is dark enough. Add more coffee if it's not. I often make the mix too dark on purpose—then rinse the fabric out in plain cool water. This way the dye comes out a little unevenly, adding an authentic touch. If you're going to put your dyed material in the wash afterward, stain the fabric very dark and wash it (by itself) in cold water, so that most of the color comes back out. After several launderings you may have to freshen the tint—this is *not* a fixed dye. If you can get away with laundering in cool water without soap, the effect will last longer.

Sometimes, particularly on a valance with a tassel fringe, I'll go back over the edges or tips with very thick instant coffee mixed with just a little warm water. This darkens the edge nicely and creates a more authentic appearance. In fact, if the overall color of the fabric is good, this final touch may be all you need.

If your fabric is mostly natural fibers—cotton, linen, silk—it's likely to take the coffee dye well. Some rayons will, too. Nylon, acetate, or polyester may not. If the fabric is a blend, you may get an interesting slubbed or shadowed effect as the fibers take the dye at different rates, but if you're feeling cautious, test a corner of the fabric first. Obviously, this technique can't be used on fabrics that absolutely have to be dry-cleaned. Wool and some rayons may shrink in water, as will new unbleached muslin. But the beauty of the Attic look is that you don't really have to worry about it! With all that stuff around, no one will notice short curtains, shrunken pillowcases, or overly stained fabrics. Just do it and get it done. It's all about texture, age, and disheveled charm anyway. Stains, tears, and mistakes—as well as pulls, nicks, scratches, and chips—only add to the ambience. A spilled wineglass is no big deal. In this setting, you can *relax*.

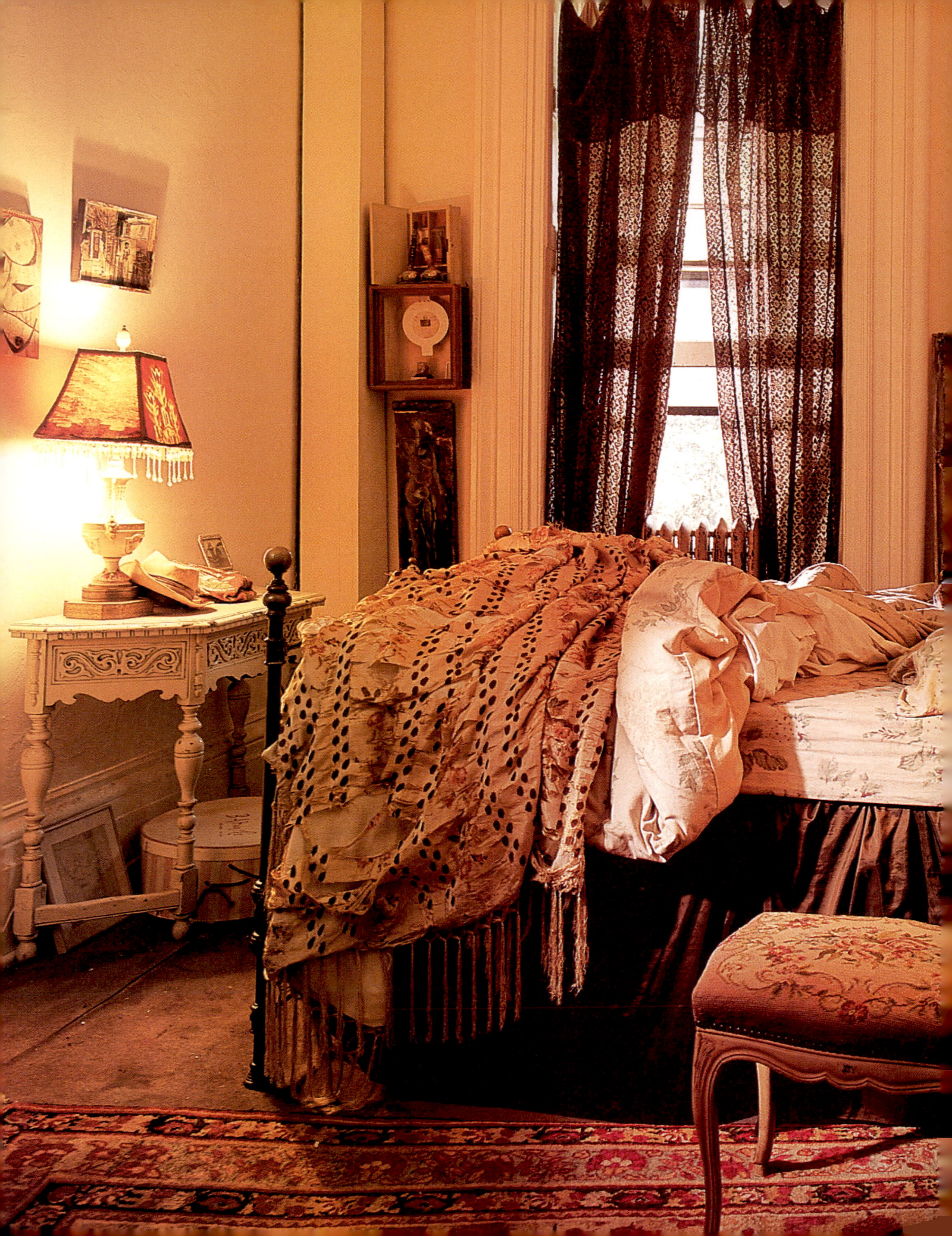

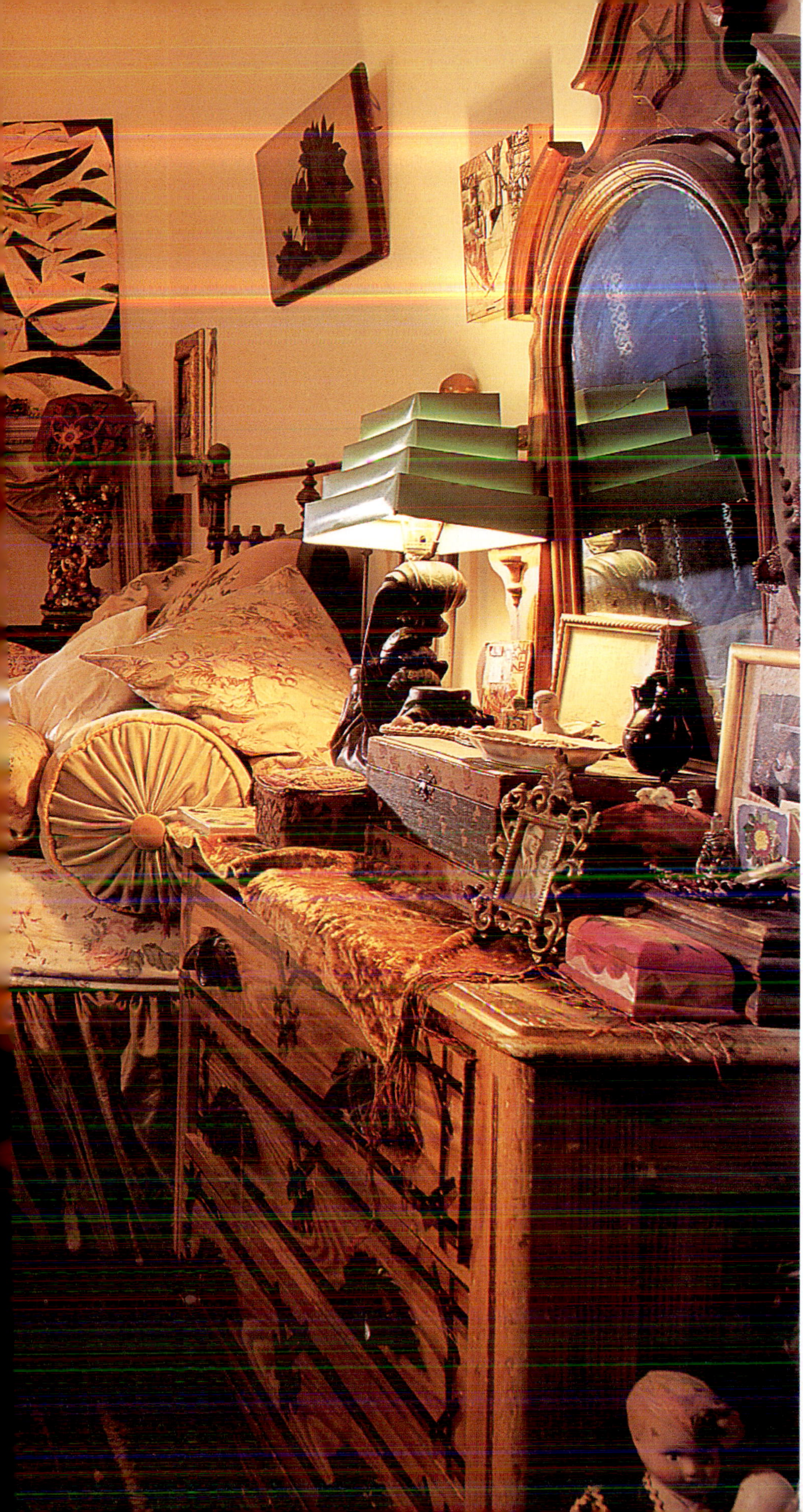

The vanity in the bedroom is a nice cottage piece bought at a shop in Connecticut; the demilune table against the wall to the left was a junky 1970s reproduction. It was painted with cream-colored enamel and left out in the yard so long it developed a terrific aged patina. The iron-and-brass bed was found at a neighborhood tag sale for an incredible $15. You often find these bedsteads covered with layers of white paint; this one looks great stripped down to the bare metal.

A major inspiration for this setting is the look and feel of the French Quarter in New Orleans—its gorgeously decaying architecture linked indelibly with the harlequin images of Mardi Gras. Here a decadent swag of pink silk (purchased at a Manhattan drag shop) frames vintage furnishings in gently faded jewel tones. The clarets, bottle greens, and dusty roses popular in yesterday's upholstery fit in well here. Stately window treatments are another key element.

A casually bedded-down collection of dolls draws the eye like a magnet. A beautiful old doll is like a piece of figurative sculpture, and has some of the aura and presence of a statue. This collection, which started with childhood keepsakes, shows that character counts. Dolls that are expressive, well-worn, and even a little crusty have a strong anima; dolls that are pristine and fussy, on the other hand, scream "gift shop" and will turn any room that harbors other Victorian objects into something sticky-sweet.

Aging Using Ash If you're aging cotton, muslin, string, or cotton trim and you want a really stained, mildewed, outside-in-the-elements look, stain it with the coffee mix and sprinkle some ashes over it while it's still wet. Let it sit until it's about half dry, then rinse quickly in cool water. I use this same technique to age labels, picture mats, and plain white paper for use as stationery. Skip the rinse—just brush off any loose particles after the paper is dry. Even pencil looks good on crusty, aged paper—and typewriter type looks amazing!

Drapes, Curtains, and Other Window Treatments

The softening effect of fabric and textiles is key in Attic, and if you're creating *any* environment that's Victorian in feel or otherwise luxurious or baroque, drapes or curtains are crucial.

There are dozens of styles, however, and seemingly endless ways to hang them. Will you put the rod inside the window, on the molding, outside the molding, above it, all the way up to the ceiling? Do you need those sheers? What the hell are they for, anyway? I find curtains to be a particularly perplexing problem for most people (I get confused myself), but they add an important element of comfort to a home that you can't get any other way.

Yes, if you're doing the open, clean thing (as in Chapter Two, "Spare," for example), the rule may not apply, but at least put curtains up in your bedroom. Surely the feeling of comfort, not to mention privacy, is needed there. Do you live in an apartment that faces another apartment? You'll want the option of closing your curtains. Does your window face a brick wall or look down on a used car lot? This calls for sheers or semisheers, which will let light in but mercifully blur the view. Do you hate bright sunlight in the bedroom? You'll want heavy curtains that close. If you need to cover an air conditioner for effect but expose it for function, you'll want a tieback or finial. If there is a radiator beneath the windowsill, you will need either to cut your curtain above it or make sure your rod extends well past the sides of the radiator so it clears it. If you want to swag the curtains with finials or tiebacks, make sure you have enough fabric to cover at least double the width of the window. Using tiebacks and finials for purely utilitarian purposes does not require extra fabric. But if you're doing something stylish, it's critical to have the volume the extra fabric provides.

How to Make Small Windows Look Larger How else do you narrow the field? A few thoughts: First, take a good look at all the windows in the room. If you have dinky windows and you want to make them look larger, maybe there's room to extend a rod past the molding on either side, making the window appear wider. If one of the windows slams right up against a side wall, however, you'll have to hang the rods *inside* the molding. If you want grand, dramatic swagged curtains and don't have tall windows, you can fake it by hanging the curtains well above the window frame—up to the ceiling, if need be. Just make sure that the swag is deep and thick enough to conceal the bare wall above the window.

Budget Yourself Before you decide anything, think about how much you can spend. Dramatic curtains use a lot of fabric, and even relatively inexpensive fabrics can add up to a fair amount of money. If you decide to have elaborate draperies made, you'll pay hundreds of dollars. If you prefer to do them yourself, you'll pay less, but it will still be a significant investment. Prepare yourself by making an estimate. If you really want to create a big hooshed and swagged floor-length drape, count on four to six times the length and twice the width in yardage—12 to 16 yards for one 3-foot-wide window. Do you have three windows and $50? We haven't even considered hardware! Get the picture?

Try to be realistic and know what you're getting into with your money and your time.

Once you've done your reality checks, cruise some home magazines. *World of Interiors* contains classic, time-worn examples. Pick out the treatments you like. Will they work in your house, and with your budget? Curtains are key in almost all vintage settings, so set aside the money for the fabric even if you have to skimp on other furnishings. If you find some great old drapes at a thrift store, you're in luck. All you need are some nice rods and rings. I prefer black iron, over the fat wooden rods with "bagel" rings. There are stores, such as ABC Carpet & Home in New York, that have great, inexpensive selections of hardware.

The subdued jewel tones that add spunk to the interior turn brilliant, like stained glass, on a sunlit porch. Here exposure to the elements requires keeping things simple, but color fills the space visually.

Choosing Fabrics

Three things are important in choosing fabrics:

1. *Don't* buy cheap-looking fabric. Try to find something that feels natural and looks authentic—not fabrics pretending to be something they're not,

Notice how the Chinese lanterns fill out the corner and the low-hung painting incorporates an old coffee table that displays a collection of cherished boxes. The large mirror brings together the disparate smaller wall objects and creates the apex of a triangle for the hoosh below. The textiles displayed here include a beaded dress from the 1920s and a vintage lingerie bag.

like fake printed moiré, or something with a horrible excuse for gold thread in the weave, or crispy-bright versions of old Victorian prints. Real vintage prints and successfully faded ones are fine. Natural fabrics and woven-in patterns (jacquards and real moiré) are nearly always safe choices, but run a mile from flame stitch—ouch!

Silk organza is beautiful and isn't terribly expensive—you can find it at around $10 a yard. The colors are often exquisite (even without coffee-staining). Real linen is always fine. Old linen tablecloths can be reasonable if they aren't too fancy, and they come already finished. Rayon taffeta isn't unreasonable, and sometimes you can find brocades, jacquards, rayon velvet, or cotton velveteen on sale. These all have an authentic look. Wool flannel suiting can make fabulous drapes as well. Do shop around—fabrics vary wildly in price. I've seen plain sand-colored linen for $7 a yard at one place and $50 at another! Large stores featuring discounted fabrics are usually the best bet; if the shop is too exclusive-looking, it will be expensive.

2. Before you make your final selection, roll some of the fabric off the bolt and feel it. Is it supple or stiff? Gather it up loosely in your hand to see how gracefully it falls, how easily it will gather or pleat. If you want a flat valance or panel, does it have enough body not to look flimsy? Be sure to hold an end up to a window or light to see what it looks like with light filtering through. As often as not, a hidden pattern in the weave is going to show up, and if you don't like it, you're going to hate the drapes in the daytime.

3. If it's a washable fabric, wash it before you make and hang the drapes; if it's going to shrink at all, you want to shrink it before you cut and hem it, but you also want to make the material relax a little. This applies to ready-made panels as well: even if you press them a little afterward to get out the heavy creases, they'll still be more relaxed and graceful after washing than brand-new fabric, which can look stiff and awkward and take months to settle down.

Hardware and Hanging

There are dozens of ways to hang curtains. I love seeing a lot of fabric just draped over and down, but this takes yards and yards of material and can double your expenses. Black wrought-iron rings are nice for panels, as are old curtain rings (they don't have to match) or plain brass rings from the hardware store (but please, tone down the brass with one of the aging techniques in Chapter Seven). Wooden rings, if they're narrow, can be immersed in a *very* watered-down mix of black and raw umber paint to stain them and make them look weathered. Most wooden rings have a smaller ring attached that's supposed to be sewn onto the curtain. To avoid the sewing, buy some of the old-fashioned drapery hooks—you know, the kind made for those awful pinch-pleat things you see over equally awful sliding glass doors. They're very cheap, and you can simply push the pointed end up through the top of the fabric and hook the hook through the small ring.

As for finishing off the fabric, I just leave the selvage edge as is, and hem the tops and bottoms with a double-rolled seam so no raw edges are seen on either side. If the drape is long enough to puddle, and the fabric doesn't easily fray, you can even skip hemming the lower edge. If you really hate sewing, you can also take the panels to a dry cleaner—some cleaners will hem them inexpensively.

VALANCES

Valances are a great way to add a layer of interest to your windows. Here are three simple valances.

A SCALLOPED VALANCE

One of my favorite tricks is to turn a smaller piece of vintage fabric into a flat valance. They're quick and easy to make, even if your tailoring skills are nil.

You can use this treatment to add a little drama to an otherwise bare window, or use it with curtains, shades, wooden shutters, or blinds. The best part is that it hides all your curtain hardware, so you can use any cheap thing you want (remembering, of course, that it will show on the outside).

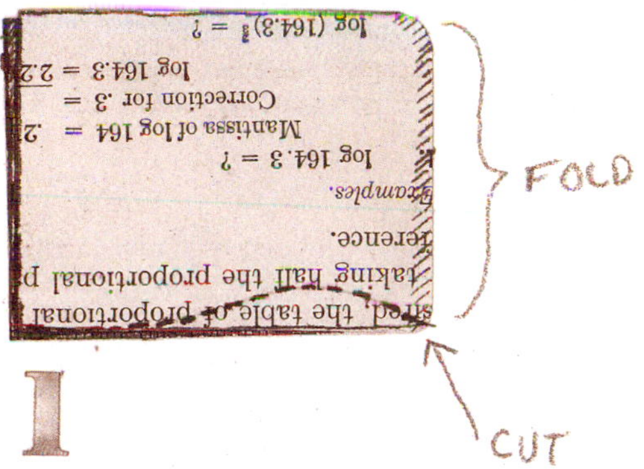

Step 1: Start by measuring across the top of the window and buying an expandable tension rod to fit. You'll need a width of fabric at least 2 inches wider than the window, and from 1/4 to 3/4 yard long. Mark and trim the piece so that you have a rectangle 2 inches wider than the rod and 3 inches deeper than the depth you want on the finished valance. A 9-inch depth will give you a 6-inch drop, and normally you'll want at least that. A 12- to 14-inch drop will be more dramatic.

Step 2: Remember how you learned in school to fold a piece of paper in half and cut out a heart? You use the same principle here. Fold the fabric in half so that the sides meet, put a few pins in it to keep it in place, mark what will be the bottom edge with a curve or scallop, then cut through both layers. Open it out, and you'll have a decorative, symmetrical edge. (If you prefer, of course, you can leave the bottom edge straight.)

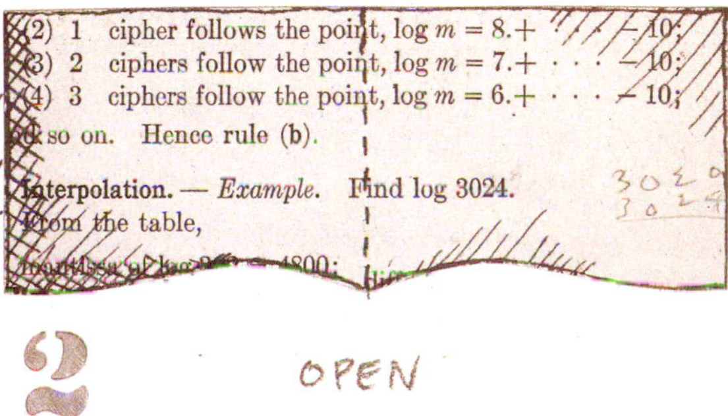

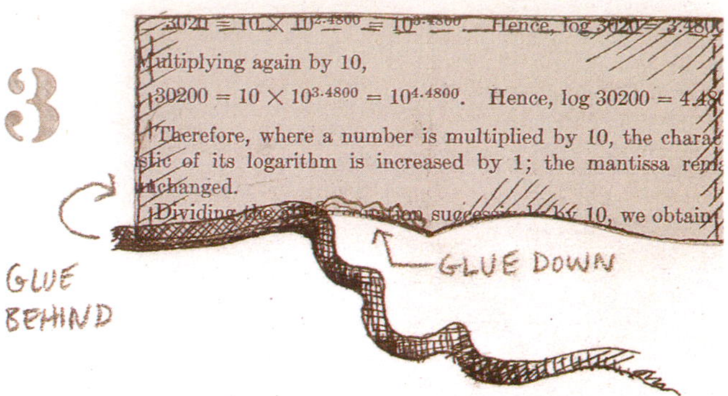

Step 3: Turn back the side edges and stitch them down, then stitch a pocket for the rod along the top. This can be done pretty quickly by hand if you don't have a sewing machine, or you can use iron-on seam tape or fabric glue. Just remember that depending on the thickness and weave of the fabric, sunlight may cast telltale shadows wherever you leave big blobs of glue or bunched-up fabric. (I used cotton damask and didn't need to worry about it.)

Step 4: Trim with a length of welting, braid, or fringe. For a deeply curved or scalloped edge, you'll need a length of trim that's 1½ to 2 times the width of the valance. Use fabric glue or a hot-glue gun to secure the trim along the edge, letting the trim extend ¼ inch or so below the cut edge of the fabric. After this has set, turn the raw edge of the trim to the back and glue it down.

Step 5: Finally, add a tassel, button, or appliqué in the center, if you like, then thread the rod through the pocket and pop the valance into the top of your window.

A word of caution: Hot glue can be hard to control, so be careful. For working with fabric and small projects, try to find a glue gun with a small nozzle that will give you a reasonably fine bead. One of the problems with hot glue is that it has a tendency to come out in fat globs. If you forget what you're dealing with and dab at it with your finger, it will stick to your skin and burn like the dickens. I've found that if I lick my finger and pat it down very quickly—sort of the way you'd test a hot iron—the glue won't burn or stick.

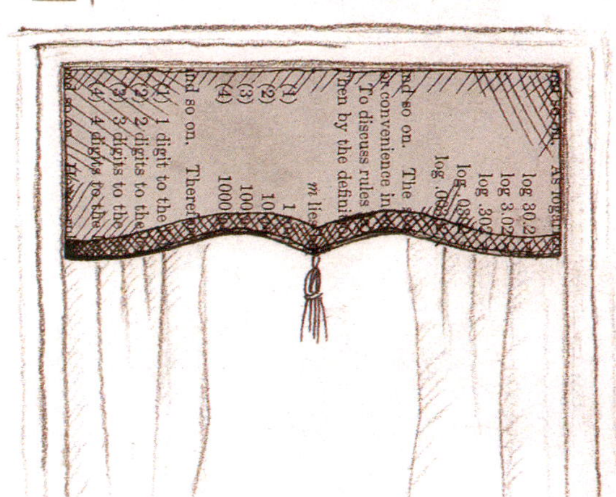

FOLDED PANEL VALANCE

Luckily, windows are often the same width as fabrics, which generally range from 42 to 60 inches. If you can match a width with the width of your windows, you can make an effective but very simple fold-over panel. Choose a fabric that looks good on both sides and buy a length 1½ times as long as the window, measured on the inside.

Step 1: Sew or hot-glue your chosen trim along the edge at one end. Do the same on the opposite (under) side. Turn and tack the ends of the trim to the back for a clean edge.

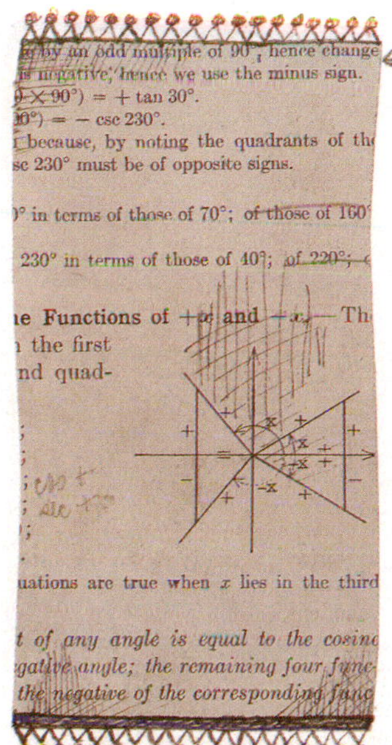

Step 2: Fold the panel over the tension rod, back to front. The top panel of fabric will form a sort of valance. Since there will be twice as much fabric behind as in front, you may have to take measures to keep the panel from sliding—especially if the fabric is slippery. Double-sided carpet tape along the top of the rod will hold it in place.

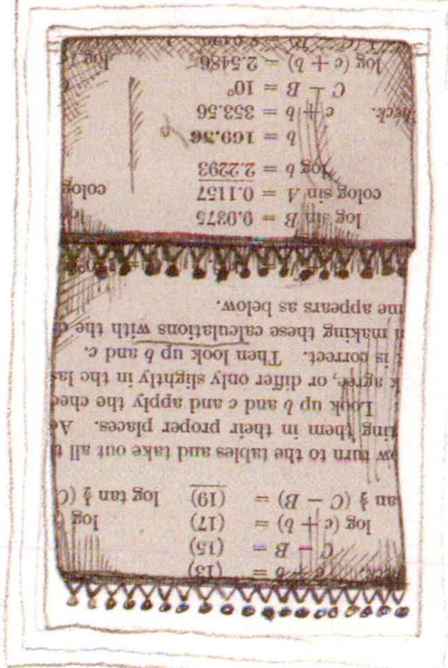

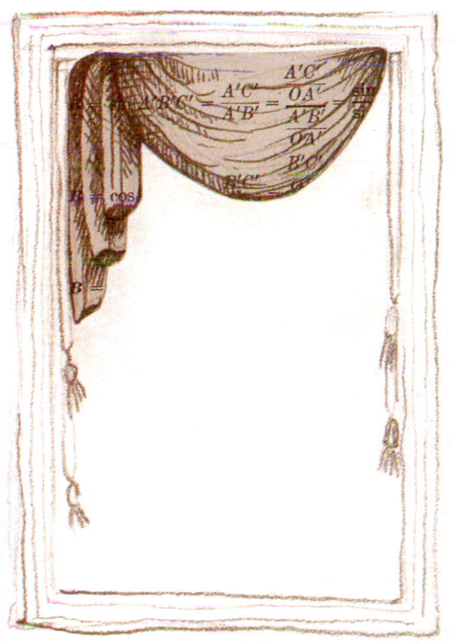

SHAWL VALANCE WITH RIBBON TASSEL

An especially easy-to-make valance is to simply drape a large silk shawl scarf over a tension rod. Tie tassels to the ends of a couple of lengths of ribbon (each a yard or two long), and tie or pin them around either end of the rod.

[Two: *Spare*]

Pages 28–29
Rather than setting it on a table, the owner has mounted this old printer's cubby on a pair of sturdy brackets so that it floats a foot or so above the floor—breaking a plane in an unusual way and helping to make the important floor-to-ceiling connection. Above the cubby, a light-box landscape from the 1950s is an amusing twist on the theme of nature contained. In this respectful setting, it's kitsch art supreme—and actually quite lovely with its warm glow and dreamy vista.

These antique animal figures are made primarily from natural materials. Neither quite toy nor sculpture, they were chosen because of their expressiveness and unusual realism.

Careful construction and particularity can make otherwise ordinary things worth framing. This strange and beautiful pair of work gloves—the gauntlets seal fur, the palms leather—have been so shaped by the wearer they've almost become hands themselves (the title: "Manual").

Right: Jeffrey's brush collection is incredible in this setting—the alcove shelf. It was very narrow and a row of tiny statues, vases, and so on were not part of the concept in this house. Brushes were ideal: narrow, diverse, and in every shape imaginable. Each personality was allowed to shine.

Attic may be an artful jumble of great trash; not so Spare. In the Spare decor, each furnishing and object is surrounded by space, framed by it, as if it were on display in a gallery—whether it's an actual piece of artwork, a lamp, or a found object. Here the fewer pieces you have, the more beautiful each must be.

It may seem a contradiction in terms, but the no-clutter Spare scheme is a very good setting for the repetitive collection—the sort that runs in a single genre. If you only have eyes for copper pots or antique farm implements, Spare may be your mode. Attic is grand for the omnivorous collector; Spare is a great venue for the passionately focused. One of the most pleasing and arresting displays in this home is of old whisk brooms and brushes, lined up in a niche of shelves. That's all there is to it—old brushes and brooms, displayed in all their common and curious shapes, worn by use and accident. The effect is extraordinarily tactile. Straw and camel hair and boar bristles, bundled in rows, repeated and multiplied. Repetition and pattern bring this homely object into sharp focus, in all its mysterious *thing*ness.

Call it a kind of Zen: Spare is about the thingness of things, whether it is the beautiful, singular piece or the single object in its multiple incarnations.

Jeffrey Jenkins is an artist and graphics designer who creates starkly beautiful assemblages using such natural elements as sod, pressed earth, and tree bark—as well as glass, wood, and paper artifacts that have been so weathered by the elements that they're halfway back to nature. His habits as a collector have nothing to do with chasing bargains: this is all about discovery, and finding recurring themes, textures, and designs in the surrounding environment. That environment includes fields, forests, tide lines—even road shoulders and parking lots.

Yet the first impression you get when you enter Jeffrey's home is how open, clean, and serenely spacious it feels. Once part of a dairy farm in upstate New York, the house retains the character and simplicity of a turn-of-the-century farmhouse. There's a sense of calm and generous proportion here—not to say that Jeffrey plays it safe. There are surprises everywhere. In the bedroom, for example, your eye is drawn to a dramatic black-and-white photograph in a plain black frame—and then to the red plastic monkey perched on top.

The closer you look, the more you see. Tucked on shelves and sometimes simply nailed to the wall are all sorts of curiosities—fossils, metals, grasses, fur. Here is a row of transparent boxes, each displaying a single, oddly beautiful animal or mineral specimen. And over there a box full of fibrous shapes that turn out to be what Jeff calls "road kill" pinecones; they've been run over so many times they've become two-dimensional. The most beautiful ones are displayed in Riker boxes on a chest in the upstairs room.

Style here is subtly pervasive and very personal. Jeffrey's art, like his collections, expresses a coherent theme: in his words, "the blurred intersection between the works of nature and those of humans."

"Nature contained" is one of the ways he describes his approach. By putting a familiar natural element into a starkly simple framework, he leads the viewer to see it from a renewed perspective—so that the identity of the material speaks for itself and by itself, allowing the viewer to reexperience it. Through his eyes I realized I was seeing things in an altogether different way than I'd ever seen them before—a world of seemingly mundane things that had always been there, patiently waiting to be noticed. It was like a new category of seeing: I no longer thought of alligators as totems of Florida, but as animals with a repetitive pyramidal texture. A trip to the Metropolitan Museum was completely turned around: instead of gawking at the pharaoh's gilded sarcophagus, I gazed in wonder at a browned scrap of linen in a frame—a bit of woven fabric that had been used to wrap a mummy. Weathered rectangular signs with the lettering worn away became abstract art, not faded advertisements, and a view of some pretty woods bisected by a single telephone line became a vista as perfect as a sunset.

My attempts to describe this singular vision fall short of experiencing it, but the point is that you can discover some marvelous things literally along the side of the road. Pinecones, dried weeds, tree bark, homemade tools—exquisite patterning and strong design can be found both in nature and in humble man-made things. Witness those wonderful whisk brooms: great collectibles can turn up in the most unlikely places. Look around—you may discover things you love at your own doorstep.

Strong natural patterns and textures are brought into sharp focus in this Spare bedroom. The artful works of nature are framed in the simplest possible way, so that the framing doesn't get in the way of the objects themselves. Even the titles of these pieces are kept simple. On the dresser, the larger glass-and-wood box, meticulously filled with bamboo except for a narrow parting that runs from front to back, is called "Path." The metal box on the wall to its left displays grasses pressed against a porthole window; in front of it a tree root arches up more than 5 feet and joins an old die once used to hand-cast railroad parts. It's titled "Route."

Keys to Spare

Keep the mood genial and a little offbeat. Bold and masculine is an appropriate mood for Spare, and it's a prime setting for serious art. But if you don't want your home to look like a corporate lounge, avoid the slick look. Marble is fine if it's real. Fake marble is out of the question, however, and black leather and glass are total clichés. Steer clear of Maurice Villency and monstrous plants.

Steal ideas from galleries and from other eras and cultures. Spare represents a kind of livable, workable art gallery, so take a look at the space itself the next time you visit a gallery or museum. Paintings and interiors from other eras or cultures offer more sources of inspiration for the Spare scheme: Japanese gardens and interiors, American Shaker dwellings, European monasteries, New England schoolhouses, Adirondack cottages—each tradition has its own approach. You may find inspiration in a painting by Vermeer or in a whitewashed Spanish mission. Take cues from what you collect.

Pay attention to the whole room. Even in a Spare interior, it's a mistake to ignore that frequently overlooked stretch of wall between shoulder level and the ceiling (see more under Planes). Take a good look at the room's "bones," and play up any interesting architectural elements. If the room doesn't have any, you can import some. Old pillars and salvaged porch columns may have become familiar props in decorating magazines, but as long as they're the real thing, they still look cool.

Think big. Tall, massive pieces of furniture—a beautiful old armoire or painted chest, for examples—lend themselves well to the Spare approach, helping to connect the planes of the room and becoming strong focal points that will anchor a bare-bones scheme in a grand way. A clutch of dinky pieces in a big, bare space is going to look sad—spindly orphans huddled in a cave.

Consider your personal habits as a collector. Spare assumes a high quality of attention. If you're keenly attentive, habitually neat, and a little compulsive, Spare may be your element.

Grouped as a pleasing whole, the Spare bedroom, while not ornate, can still have a sense of fullness. Paying attention to all levels and surfaces of the room will create this feeling without the clutter. Here architecture itself lends a hand. The beams and tiny upper window fill in the apex of a triangle beautifully.

Here is a wonderful homage to brushes. Simply attached to a row of nails to the wall, each brush is seen in its unique style and character. The drawing table is neatly adorned with a sample of roof shingles encased in a sheet of plastic pockets. Again, texture as element turns this into an extraordinary object instead of a selling tool.

Shaping a Spare Interior

Like a Japanese garden, the Spare approach requires careful attention to the empty or *negative* space that surrounds and showcases your furnishings. What shapes do these spaces take? Where do they lead the eye? Here, a stretch of bare floor may stop at the foot of a sculpture; there, a shadowy turn down a hallway may give a glimpse of something intriguing hanging on the wall. In a bare-bones scheme, the negative space of a doorway is fully as much a design element as a piece of furniture or a painting. This is true in any interior design, but it's acutely apparent in Spare. Clearly, an architecturally interesting space is a great candidate for the Spare approach, but you can import architectural interest, too—with elements brought in from your local salvage yard.

Planes

A sense of spaciousness is a hallmark of the Spare decor, but you want a room to look serene and comfortable—not skimpy, cold, and underfurnished. The difference between the two will be determined by how much attention you pay to each of the *planes* of the room. This is one of the first, most basic aspects of any good design—and perhaps the most frequently overlooked.

Strictly speaking, the planes of a room include the floor, the ceiling, and the four vertical walls that connect them, enclosing the interior like a box. Within the box, you've got furnishings that may range from a coffee table that's lower than knee height to a bookcase that rises to the ceiling. Unfortunately, many of the rooms I see exist only below the waist, with the upper half totally ignored. Take a look at your room: Does everything except a lone picture stop at the height of your sofa? I know, bare is cool, but bare doesn't mean barren. Look at the interior of the living room on pages 38–39. As Spare as it is, each plane is addressed.

Addressing all the planes of a room isn't complicated. Think of it in terms of flat surfaces—floor, walls, ceiling—enclosing a big cube of space. Then visually divide that cube into three or four horizontal sections. These need to be connected to each other visually as well. *Connecting* the planes and *breaking* them are related concepts: breaking a plane means interrupting a surface—hanging a picture on an expanse of wall, for example, or bridging different surfaces, such as by hanging draperies which connect the floor to the ceiling.

What's on your walls? Does anything visually connect the floor with the ceiling? Floor-to-ceiling connections will make an enormous difference, not only in terms of pulling your design scheme together but in the perceived *size* of your interior. A room of average height that's furnished only up to the shoulders can feel clamped down and even oppressive. If you want to open it up, lay claim to its upper reaches. Even a nice high ceiling will go unappreciated if you do nothing to tie it to the rest of the room. And a *very* high ceiling over bare walls will give you the drafty ambience of an airplane hangar! Whether you've got 7 feet of headroom or 14, the floor-to-ceiling connection is crucial.

Window treatments, including draperies that extend above and below the actual window, are an obvious way to make the floor-to-ceiling connection, but in the Spare scheme pictured in this chapter, the privacy of the countryside allows for bare windows. Whether or not you're using drapes, you can and should bring other elements into play. Tall bookcases, large paintings, framed collections, as well as chandeliers, hanging birdcages, floor lamps, columns, folding screens, ladders—even an old garden gate or door leaning against the wall can become an architectural element that will help make the vertical connection.

Look at the room again. What occupies the center of the cube? You can let most tall, massive pieces hug the walls, but use the middle ground, too, allowing furniture like low sofas and tables to "float." (More on this in Chapter Six, "Alienated.") And don't be afraid to send up a floor-to-ceiling item anywhere in the room, if it works.

Whether the room is a shoebox or an airplane hangar, if you want it to feel serenely proportioned and comfortably spacious, pay attention to all its dimensions. If you marry the visual planes of the room to each other, and think in terms of items that are knee high, waist high, shoulder high, over the head, and at the ceiling, and include something at each level, you will inevitably create a more balanced, inviting, and relaxed environment.

Hooshing Repetitive Collections

The Spare scheme in this chapter shows a number of great ways to hoosh repetitive collections. If your collectibles can be hung flat, hang them directly on the wall like pictures. If they can't be easily hung, try lining them up on top of the wainscoting or picture molding or even on top of a doorframe. If you don't have wainscoting, nail a shallow shelf or molding across one or more walls at about shoulder height.

Another of Jeffrey's categories—small metal objects, collected for their peculiarity; by themselves they would disappear, but as a collection they set the mood to wander. These are simply displayed on a windowsill using the forest as a perfect backdrop.

Bookcases, cubbyholes, and shelves are naturals, of course, but pay attention to the planes here, too. Don't line up a row of tiny objects along a shelf with nothing but air between one shelf and the next. In typical bookshelves, with a foot or so between each shelf, you can lean framed pictures and small paintings (as well as trays and plates) against the back wall—or use pushpins to tack up unframed prints, photos, and small collectibles. This is an easy and appealing way to pull together a shelf full of small, odd-size pieces. And don't forget the top shelf: large items that reach toward the ceiling will add height and importance to the whole unit.

A simple, massive, built-in cupboard and painted wood floors are traditional elements of cottage style; they make a pleasing backdrop for this Spare scheme. If you have a badly botched-up wood floor or one that's been painted "landlord's brown," consider giving it a lift with a couple of coats of white or pale blue porch paint. Top it with a coat or two of low-gloss varnish to postpone repainting. A bit laborious—but easier than refinishing, and cheaper and more appealing than wall-to-wall carpet.

Above the eight-legged mahogany table, a piece of deeply grooved tree bark is mounted behind the lid of an old oak school desk—this one bearing an engraved ruler across the top edge. A beaded-board ceiling and stripped wood wainscoting add more natural pattern and texture to the room.

Right: When they're filled with great stuff, even plastic boxes can find a home in a good hoosh. In the artist's studio, shelves hold plastic storage boxes filled with old hand-repaired books, bits of fur, bark, twigs, and decayed and weathered finds both from the local woods and from the owner's travels in the West and South. Oddities from antiques shops include a case of artificial teeth, all of them numbered, and a deer-foot thermometer. Endless combinations of handmade and manufactured goods from an earlier time, all of them priceless.

DIY Art

DIY (Do-It-Yourself) is a familiar enough term that has been given new meaning by serious artists who have found alternative venues for their work outside the big, established galleries. Even if you can't draw a stick figure you can create and frame effective pieces to decorate your walls. Abstract art, Dada, Julian Schnabel's broken plates—the definition of art has expanded. I think it's fabulous: it means that nearly everyone can make his own. Maybe not the sort that other people will buy, but that's another story. If you have a mind to, you can make art for yourself.

Framing and Matting Images

There are endless possibilities, but for the sake of spurring you on, I'm going to offer some ideas for framed and matted images.

Start with bits of paper and materials that are interesting in themselves. One place to find good stuff is in old framed pictures or photos. Old mats, old bits of cardboard and newspaper, *really* stained papers—sometimes even the backs of the photos themselves look good. Choose a piece that's big enough to fill the frame you've selected, glue on a couple of odd scraps of red paper, and maybe add a circle of paint. You can use the lid of the paint can to stamp it on, or do it freehand. Let all the elements be rough. Scrub in a patch of white paint—the brush should be almost dry so that it looks scrumbly. Let that dry and then do a quick rough sketch or scribble some words over it with a soft pencil. Don't worry about the quality of the drawing or try to make the circle perfect. The combination of old, stained components and just a touch of something roughed in by hand is what creates the effect. If what you've done looks at all interesting and old, it'll look *great* framed and matted.

If you really don't want to attempt anything freehand, choose a simple sketch or picture you like from a book or magazine (don't like it too much—it'll get wrecked). Trace the picture onto gently stained cardboard with transfer paper, available at art supply stores—Saral's "graphite gray" looks just like pencil. Once again, don't try to make things perfect: firm, quick strokes generally look best, so don't worry about following every line exactly.

RICHMOND STRAIGHT CUT No1 CIGARETTES
LUXENE

Some Other Ideas

Idea 1: Try writing or sketching directly on the back of the glass in a picture frame, using a grease pencil; mount it over an old clipping or print. (Look at Tapies, Cy Twombly, or Picasso collages for inspiration.)

Idea 2: If you've got scraps of tattered but beautiful lace, embroidery, or other textiles, try mounting them against a background of colored cardboard, old wallpaper or marbled book paper, a larger piece of velvet or silk—whatever creates a pleasing contrast and ties in with your room's palette. Let each scrap float in the center of the backing, attaching it only as necessary with a couple of stitches or minute dabs of glue. Be sure to leave the edges ragged—if they're very frayed around the borders, all the better. This is a great way to salvage a memory from keepsake clothing or linens that are falling apart. When the composition is done, frame it behind glass.

Idea 3: You can even frame small articles whole. That elaborate christening dress or those exquisite doll clothes your grandmother sewed for you can be mounted against a backing of linen, textured paper, or stained mat board. Frames with UV-filtering glass, which you can find at art or photo suppliers, will help preserve crumbling old textiles, papers, and photos.

Idea 4: Frame "found art." I find extraordinary things in all sorts of unlikely places: old ledgers with browning edges, tiny notebooks with minute listings, sewing samples pinned to faded construction paper, tie-on retail tags with handwritten prices and notes, books with pages scribbled on by children. Three black document frames, each holding a different handwritten page, would look great hung in a tight row—or just tack the pages to the wall with silver pushpins.

Consider pages from old stamp albums, and the sorts of ready-made collages you find in old scrapbooks—photographs, invitations, party favors, dried corsages, dance cards, and other memorabilia; old-fashioned black mounting corners and yellow glue stains on the page are icing on the cake. The list goes on: one of my favorite finds is an amazing set of pencil drawings in an old biology-lab workbook!

Left: In another upstairs bedroom is a wonderful old chest of drawers displaying flattened pinecones in Riker boxes—pinecones that have fallen and been run over so many times that their appearance is altered and now resembles archaic sea creatures or fossilized trilobites. These objects of wonder and beauty are completely free.

Above: The back of an old frame and a tacked-on postcard are instant art. Often the back of the frame is more interesting than the front; just add a little bit of ephemera or leave it as is.

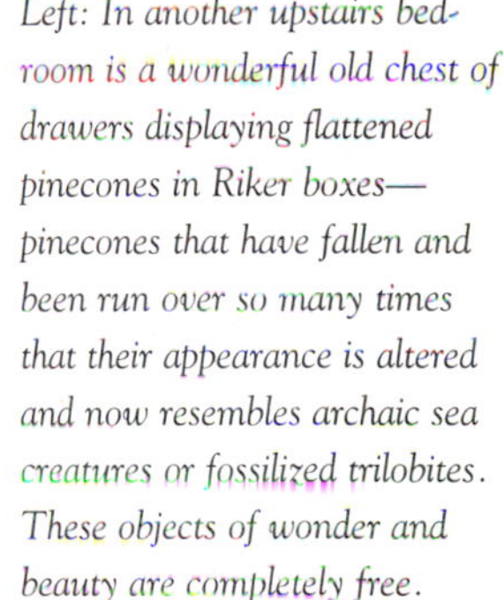

DIY FRAMING AND MATTING

Many pieces of found art look fine just hung on a hook or pinned to the wall, but there's something amazing about putting a frame around a piece. Custom framing is very expensive, however, and good, inexpensive ready-mades can be hard to find—the prices vary wildly according to the source. If you stumble on some bargains in a junk store or at the flea market, buy. Discount and dime stores usually stock inexpensive, plain black wood frames (often called document frames) and these are very versatile. Keep in mind that with the exception of frames for mirrors, those that are very ornate may overpower what you're framing. In any event, steer clear of those horrible souped-up things made of china or cheap filigree—unless of course they're *very* camp and fit in with your scheme!

MATS

A nicely beveled mat adds a great finished look to a piece of artwork, but custom matting is another expensive proposition, and even intrepid DIYers may be daunted at the prospect of cutting mat board themselves. Without a special tool, it's difficult to cut a mat with a straight, clean edge—much less a beveled one. If your frame doesn't come with a usable mat, you may be able to find a precut one the right size; almost all art supply stores carry them. Stain it with coffee for a nice yellowed look.

If you have a mat that's really ugly or that doesn't have a beveled edge, you can cover it with fabric. If you have no mat at all to start from, you can patch something together from four uniform strips of cardboard. Trim them to size and tape together at the seams with paper mailing tape, making sure your corners are square. Don't overlap the cardboard—just bridge the joints with tape, front and back. Crude, but once it's covered with fabric, who will know?

Choose fabric that isn't too thick—avoid upholstery tapestry or very thick velvet. Old linen is very nice, as is cotton velvet. Once you've selected the fabric you want to use, measure and cut it so that it's 1 or 2 inches wider than the mat all around.

Step 1: Using a glue stick, thoroughly coat the front of the mat with glue. Center the mat face down on the wrong side of the fabric, and press down firmly.

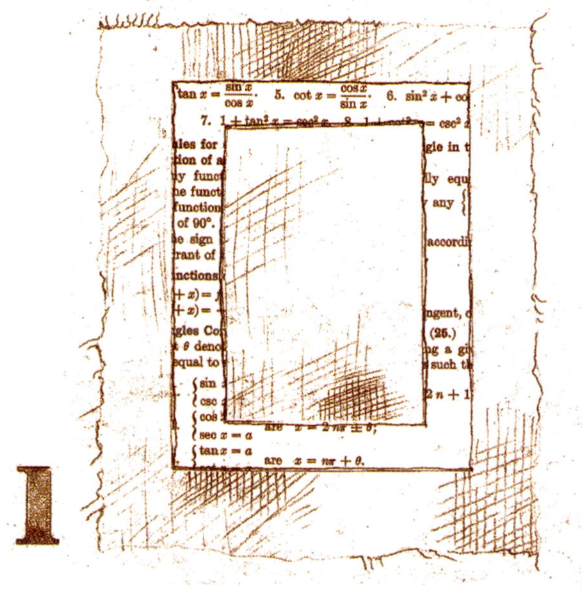

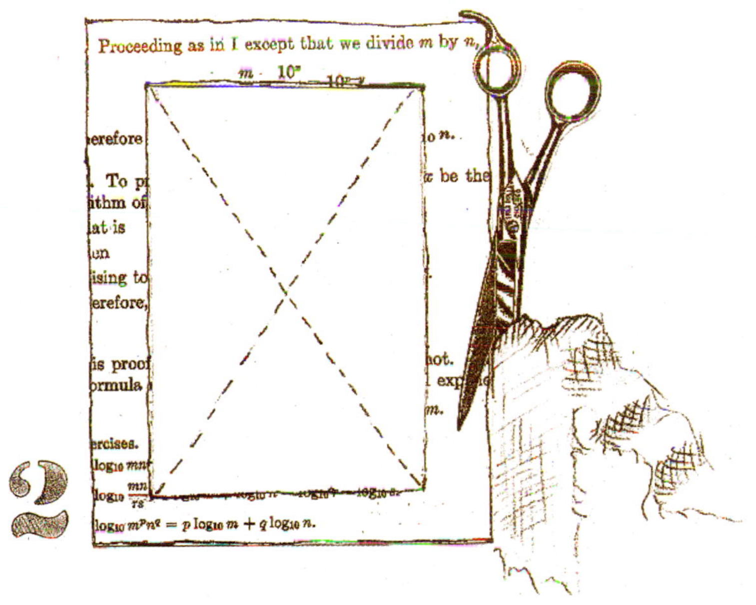

Step 2: Trim the excess fabric from the outer edges, then cut an X through the fabric inside the opening of the mat, taking the cuts right into the corners.

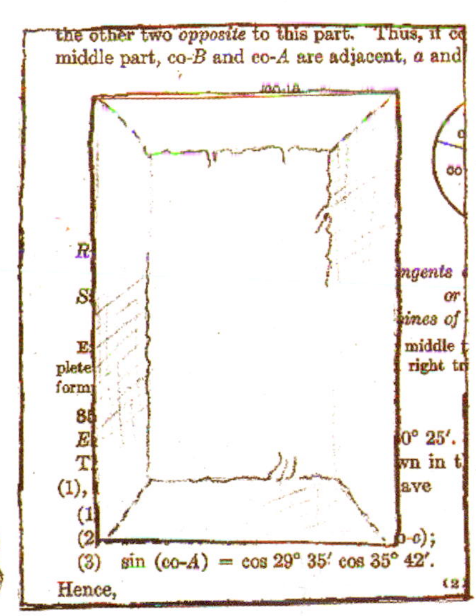

Step 3: Now trim the four triangular flaps straight across, so that each one is about 1 inch wide.

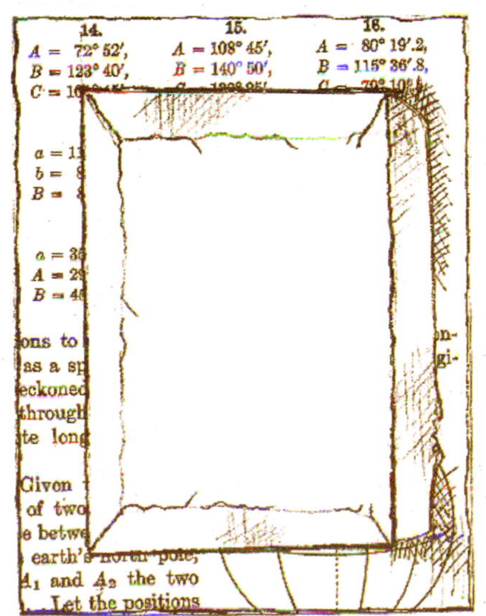

Step 4: Taking one side at a time, apply a 1-inch-wide strip of glue along the back of the mat, pull the fabric tightly over it, and press down hard, holding it in place for a few seconds until that side is set enough to move on to the next. After gluing each flap, turn the mat over to the front and check the inside corners: they should be tight and square. If the fabric isn't flush, just press it in with your thumbnail.

[Three: *Expedition*]

Pages 46–47
The antique taxidermy deer heads shown here are among the very few decorative objects made to jut straight out of the wall, breaking the plane in an unusual way. Objects that seem to emerge from a flat surface like this tease our sense of reality, suggesting some other dimension behind the wall. Tree limbs cut and arranged so that they appear to go through a wall or ceiling have the same provocative quality (see the root in Chapter Two, "Spare"). Sconces, depending on how far out they project, can give a similar effect.

Stacks of luggage and camping equipment complete the feeling of exploration. Tiny shoes are added to the hoosh—we don't know why, but it makes a story.

An Expedition space has a strong animus—it's a place with an awareness of the elements, of work and tools, a whiff of the Gothic, and animated by nature's own strange surprises. And it's warm and inviting.

Back in the 1980s, big, bare commercial spaces made over into apartments with pristine paint jobs, industrial carpeting, and a few lonely pieces of massive Italian furniture were the height of cool. Polished, austere, and impersonal, the style was the equivalent of a power suit with big shoulder pads. Photographs of those places were neat to look at, but it was always hard to imagine anyone actually living in one of them.

J. Morgan Puett and Mark Dion are postconceptual artists who have created a very different sort of big space in their Manhattan loft. Theirs is the sort of completely integrated hoosh that results from over a decade of focused, passionate collecting. Mark in particular is a dedicated amateur naturalist, and Morgan shares his enthusiasm. Their creative work includes large on-site installations that invoke both human and natural history, and their passion for the works and workings of nature is evident everywhere in their home. Together they've transformed a spacious TriBeCa loft into a fabulous habitat—and a live-in work of art.

The Expedition interior amply demonstrates how a particular collecting theme can grow into a whole world. It might have started with something as focused as a fascination with moths and butterflies or antique maps. Loaded with historic references and 19th-century atmosphere, Expedition is shaped by the owners' tastes. Yet it's easy to imagine any Edwardian-era naturalist being completely at home in rooms like these. There's an English look and feel to the style, calling up romantic associations with the best of the British Empire, its great explorers and scientists. If you've ever seen photographs of Darwin's wonderful study at Down House, Kent, you probably see echoes of it here.

Like the country home in Spare, Mark and Morgan's urban retreat fully accommodates the ongoing work of the artists who live here. Containers for natural artifacts and art supplies are an integral part of the hoosh in Jeffrey Jenkins's studio; in this more flush interior, with two artists in residence, containers are in nearly every room. Cupboards, glass boxes, trunks, suitcases, and old-fashioned cigar boxes hold prized collections and raw materials that will eventually find their way into the artists' works. As functional as they are, containers like these are beautiful collectibles in themselves—and part and parcel of what makes this space at once relaxed, workable, and splendid to look at.

Most of the furnishings in the living room are castoffs in disguise: the French provincial chair was rescued from the curb and given a custom slipcover; the wingback was bought at a junk store and recovered by a friend. A massive old office file helps to anchor the scheme. This unusual piece has drawers that pull completely out and turn on end to hold papers. The white oval labels aren't original—they're filled in with a black felt-tip—but I love that touch. Most of us have the urge to restore things to their original period condition, and latter-day "improvements" are nearly always awful. This contemporary anachronism, however, is modest and highly functional. I've grown to cherish the marks previous owners have left on vintage pieces—they form the history that makes each one unique.

Mark Dion collects flora and fauna everywhere he goes, and the cigar boxes, lined with cotton, hold exotic bugs, bones, rocks, leaves, and seashells. The extraordinary box in the dining room is an Eastlake case, a sort of Victorian diorama constructed of glass and elaborately carved wood, holding taxidermy birds perched on branches against a painted backdrop. This museum-quality case is a serious collector's piece and work of art—and one of the few single objects in their home that represents a substantial investment. Somewhat less costly are the other pieces of antique taxidermy throughout the house, and scores of inexpensive Riker boxes—displaying butterflies, dragonflies, all sorts of insect specimens—decorate nearly every room.

As it is in Spare, tools-as-sculpture is a repeated theme. In this case, the focus is on the tools a naturalist would use or collect out in the field. Hung on the wall in the dining area is a display of knives and machetes Mark has gathered during travels in Borneo, Africa, and elsewhere. In this context, inexpensive, utilitarian tools created and used by craftsmen, farmers, and fishermen become a form of folk art. Near the loft's entry, canvas bags holding camping equipment are strung together like a mobile over a stack of beautifully battered leather luggage. In

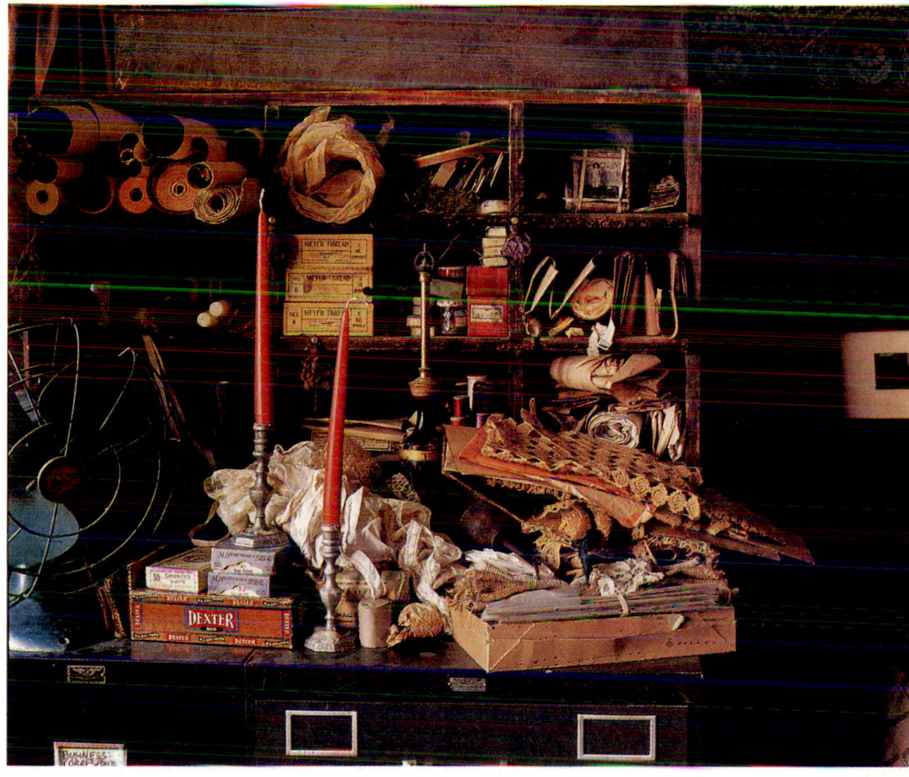

Left: The warm wood paneling in this little "front office" was found in the building's basement, part of one of the original interiors. There's a cot to recline on while you're cooking up new ideas. The light over the cot is a beekeeper's hood hung over a bulb. This is a wonderful place to work. Most of the furnishings, such as the oak file cabinet, can be found easily in antiques and used furniture stores.

Above: A well-worn cubby sitting on top of two ordinary old khaki-green file cabinets contains vintage fabrics, trims, pins, and needles. Completely utilitarian and functional, it also makes a terrific-looking hoosh.

OLD HOUSES

another corner, a cluster of vintage butterfly nets leans against the wall; in yet another, an old army cot folded and strapped with leather becomes something wonderful to look at. To put the cap on the Expedition atmosphere, Morgan completely swathed all the wall surfaces in the bedroom with canvas drop cloths, giving it the feeling of a snug tent.

In many ways, this is a scheme that pays homage to the great collections of the Museum of Natural History and the Smithsonian Institution, down to various small specimens (brought down by Morgan's cat) that are preserved in jars of formalin. The result is an endlessly fascinating "museum"—or perhaps the sort of outpost that a 19th-century gentleman-adventurer might set up for himself, hauling in by ship or camelback or elephant train his beakers and forceps, his lanterns and mosquito netting, his Oriental carpets and tins of tea. Outside the door of this urban retreat, it might as well be the Punjab.

Keys to Expedition

Explore museums, art and science magazines, period movies. Anthropological collections and natural history museums are good sources for display ideas, but you may also find inspiration in a historical shot from an old *National Geographic*. British colonial interiors (see Karen Blixen's house in Nairobi, featured in *Out of Africa*, and the interiors in *Angels and Insects*, for examples) are good settings for Expedition.

Go to the source. As with all collectibles, the objects themselves create an atmosphere you can build on. The *Carolina Science Materials* catalog is a fantastic source of vials, boxes, containers of all sorts; and the fields, the woods, the seashore, and the abandoned barn will offer all sorts of treasures to put in them. For a variety of tools and equipment, check old-fashioned hardware and junk stores as well as farm and estate sales. Sammy's in Manhattan offers antique taxidermy, as do a growing number of antiques shops across the country—haunt a few of these if they're in

The all-the-way-up-the-wall arrangement of framed art in the living room is an example of a salon-style arrangement. It's the sort of "drop dead" effect you can get when you hoosh an entire wall—especially in a room with high ceilings. The pictures are fitted together like pieces of a puzzle. The collection completely fills one vertical plane, making this big, open space feel generously furnished, even though the usual furnishings—sofa, chairs, and so on—are relatively few in number. Notice, too, how the drapery in this room is hung on a heavy rope stretched all the way across the room and a few feet forward of the window. It adds just the suggestion of a dividing line between the living and dining areas, which is enough to give a sense of separate rooms without the expense of installing drywall.

The living room furniture is gathered cozily together in a circle that floats just right of center, allowing easy movement from one part of the apartment to the next and giving a sense of spaciousness without that cavernous feeling you get in many industrial-type lofts. The hooked rug underfoot adds warmth too—one of the few remaining rug bargains among "antiques." (The table to the left of the wingback chair is actually two old bee skeps stacked one on top of the other.)

A. J. H.
A.J.H.
CLEOPATRA
FLOR DE M
Rothschilds

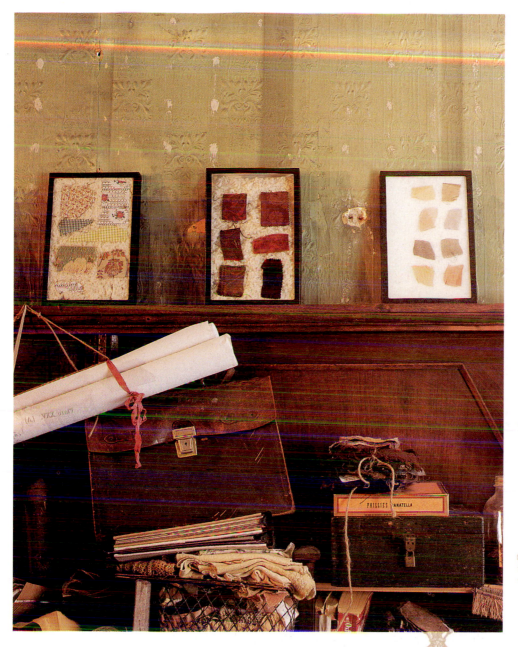

Far left: *The "triangle" is at work here. Also the top of this banquette is thoroughly filled, and the photograph of the barge creates the apex as well as adding fully to the concept.*

Left: *Pieces of fabric in frames and collages, blueprints, lace in a wire basket, a cigar box, old jars, and a weather-beaten briefcase—all bring this Expedition corner together.*

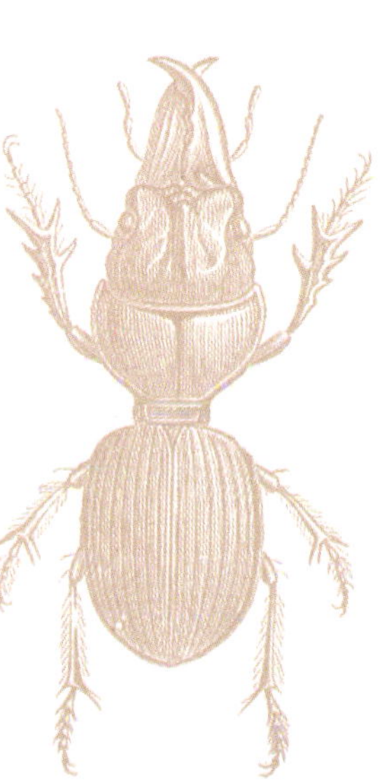

72. Coleoptera of the family of Carabidæ.

Stacked boxes are in the foreground and in the back are Mark and Morgan's collection of bug-catching nets—filling the corner and creating a sculptural effect.

your area. Even if you don't buy, their curiosities can put you in the mood.

Avoid prefabbed art. Be wary of the sorts of spanking clean and perfectly matched print-and-frame combos featured in furniture store ads. If an image has already been taken over by card stores and national hotel chains (Van Gogh's sunflowers, Raphael's angels), you don't need another reproduction in your house. Exceptions in this case are paintings, etchings, and drawings by artists with a scientific bent, such as Leonardo's anatomical drawings and inventions, Albrecht Dürer, James Audubon, and the Dutch realists. Check the print and poster bins at museum shops, and if need be, age your prints before framing. Old books are a great source for frameable images: cruise secondhand bookstores and library fund-raising sales for illustrated books on birds and wildflowers, as well as the occasional illustrated botany, zoology, biology, or anthropology text.

Hooshing a Salon-style Arrangement

One of the most fabulous things that can happen to a wall is a salon-style hanging—a large collection of framed art that reaches all the way to the ceiling. A feast for the eyes, it makes the all-important floor-to-ceiling connection and helps a large, open space like a loft feel cozily furnished. A hoosh like this has a lot of impact, but it takes a lot of pictures. A wall full of really good stuff would cost a fortune, and paintings and good prints are becoming increasingly expensive even on the flea market circuit, where "paint-by-numbers" now fetches a pretty price. And you can forget real galleries!

But there still seem to be a good number of bad paintings around at low prices, and you can sometimes find badly damaged good paintings at moderate prices. There are a number of good alternative sources for interesting frameable art listed here, but you can also salvage less-than-glorious pieces with a simple technique that will mimic the sort of smoked patina we associate with Old Masters and early 20th-century folk art.

How to Salvage Bad Art

I had one of those hokey reproduction bouquet-in-a-vase paintings, one that pictured a bunch of insipid lavender, pink, and mauve flowers—yuck! But the basic lines were okay, so I went at it with some oil paints, a black wash, and one of my favorite cure-alls—Bullseye Shellac #3. It has a great yellowy cast that looks just like aged shellac, and can be used to tone down pastel-painted furniture that's too bright or new-looking, as well as to add a

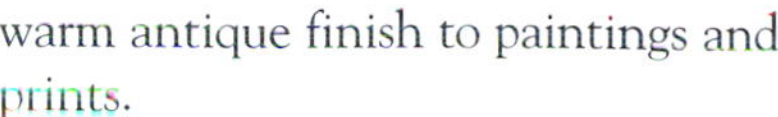

warm antique finish to paintings and prints.

For my bouquet painting, I simply took a small, cheap brush and dabbed warmer colors over the flowers. Darker oil colors (those that don't have a white base) are transparent, so the details will show through if you use the paint sparingly, but don't load up the brush. Smear the paint with your finger to lighten, if that helps.

After I'd changed all those pinks and purples into warmer shades, I let the picture dry overnight. (Rub it lightly to make sure it's dry—if the humidity is high you may need to let it dry another day.) Then use a water-based black paint in a very thin, watered-down wash, and paint over the whole image. If the wash is too dark, just dab it with a rag. The water-based black (you can use thinned acrylic or old-fashioned watercolors) *should* separate and look patchy. Let it dry, then shellac the whole surface with the Bulls-eye. Continue alternating between the wash and the shellac until you get the finish you want. I wanted a dark, slightly obscure image. This dark-wash-and-shellac treatment will give just about any picture an aged patina. If you want something a little warmer and smokier than plain black, you can experiment with the tint by mixing raw or burnt umber with the black for the wash.

Secrets to Hanging Art en Masse

How do you determine what kinds of framed art will mix well in a massed arrangement? Repetition is key in a salon-style hoosh: you can mix a lot of different elements if you have enough repetition to create a kind of pattern. There are a number of variables to consider, but for an attractive balance pay particular attention to the following: the intensity and brightness of the color in the work; the medium (pencil sketches, watercolors, etchings, oil paintings, collages); and the era or style (Renaissance, 19th century, 20th century).

Dark or intensely colored pieces will look "heavier" than pencil sketches or pale watercolors, just as large pieces will look heavier than small ones. Keep in mind the matter of perceived *weight* as you make your arrangement. Vases, lamps, or sculpture positioned against the wall should be considered part of the hoosh and taken into the balance as well.

Generally speaking, you should put the heaviest pieces toward the center of the hoosh, then work out from there. Alternatively, you can position bolder or darker images at the corners or in a row across the top to create a visual frame for the whole arrangement. Keep in mind that the row of art up at ceiling height is going to be harder to see than what's at eye level or below, so avoid putting that favorite pale pencil sketch up too high.

Setting Up Art en Masse

A good way to begin to set up your arrangement is to lay the pictures out on an expanse of bare floor or plain carpet first. Now move them around, adding and removing pieces as needed, until you get a grouping that pleases you. Use your own sense of color and balance to guide you. *Don't leave too much space between pieces.*

The bed is separated from the rest of the bedroom with drapes bought at an antiques store for about $75. This is a really sumptuous way to divide space as well as another way to break the floor-to-ceiling plane that also adds softness and a feeling of real luxury. The bed itself is made of several old ticking mattresses stacked up on a platform, with a vintage comforter and handsome handmade sheets and coverlets made of real linen and old satin.

ALWAYS KEEP REFRIGERATED
FLOR DE MELBA

Far left: This hoosh continues the idea of exploration, an arrangement of gathered and stacked finds from yards and antiques shops, coupled with handmade toy ships.

Left: The curtain on the right is the same curtain seen in the large photograph of the living room on page 50. In this close-up, we see how the curtain separates this tiny and otherwise rather useless corner into a little office nook where specimens are gathered into boxes, listed in notebooks, and arranged in stacks.

Mark and Morgan have created a cabinet of curiosities of their own—antique taxidermy, moths, and various bottled yard specimens collected by their cat.

A primary rule in a salon-style hanging is to keep approximately the same amount of space between each frame—a couple of inches on each side is about right—fitting the pieces together as if they're part of a large puzzle.

When you start hanging, make sure that the center of the grouping is at eye level or slightly below: for example, if you've got three rows of pictures, the middle row should be at eye level. Radiate out from this central grouping as you collect more art, filling in "holes" with small pieces as needed, and continuing on up to the ceiling.

Method 1: Take the pictures up one by one and hang them up roughly according to your "floor plan," knowing that you're going to get something a little different from what you started out with. Most of us will inevitably make some mistakes, however, and if you have the time and are worried about extra holes in the wall, you can proceed a little more methodically.

LARVA OF DYTISCUS MARGINALIS. CATCHING A TADPOLE.

Method 2: Make a quick, rough sketch of the layout you've created on the floor, then measure to see how much space you've left from the edge of one frame to the edge of the next, and note the measurement on your sketch. Now take the pictures up, one by one, and hang, continuing to refer to your sketch and measurements for guidance.

Method 3: An even more accurate way to assemble your pictures is to arrange your "floor plan," then trace around each frame on newsprint or wrapping paper, and cut out the paper shape. Jot a note on it to identify which picture it represents ("sketch of birds," "flower print," and so on)—otherwise with a lot of similarly sized pieces you'll forget which is which. Now fold each paper pattern exactly in half vertically to make a center crease. Unfold and tape the cutouts to the wall with masking tape, moving them around until you've got an arrangement you like. Once you've figured out how far from the top edge of a particular frame the nail—or preferably picture hook—needs to go, all you need to do is mark the spot on the center crease of the cutout, align the lower edge of the hook there, hammer the hanger nail partway in, rip the paper off, and finish tapping the nail in until the hook is snug. (Be sure to hang the actual picture before you move on to the next pattern.) The paper-cutout method is especially helpful if you're tackling this project without a buddy to assist you. Don't skip the floor plan, though—the patterns alone won't tell you how the color and style of each piece will affect the balance of the hoosh.

Framing Massed Art

Inexpensive black document frames or frames of plain dark wood will mix well

with antique and more elaborate gilt frames. As with the pictures themselves, you can use a variety of frames if each type is repeated several times in the arrangement. For example, if you've got a dozen pictures variously framed in black, gold, and wood, they'll look at home together if there are several of each style.

On the other hand, if the grouping includes art in a wide range of color intensities, styles, and periods, you may be able to pull the hoosh together by displaying each piece in the same simple mat and frame. Sometimes just changing the mat on a particular picture will make all the difference. And if you have a group that's *overly* matched—say a set of six botanical prints the same size—you can either scatter them through a larger, disparate arrangement so that they help pull the hoosh together, or you might hang the six by themselves, in six wildly different frames you've picked up at the dime store and flea market.

Play around. Don't be afraid to mix, match, try unlikely things together—remembering that a sense of balance and an element of repetition will solve all kinds of design problems.

Using Curtains as Room Dividers

Rule: Fabric hanging somewhere in a room will change the feeling of the room entirely. Curtains are an obvious starting place, but don't rule out other possibilities. In the loft in this chapter, a drape separates the living and dining areas. You may want to curtain off a small space for your home office, or, if you have a studio, separate your bedroom from your living area. Or maybe you just want to add a little drama to an interior that's on the bare side. Some drapery swagged across even a shallow niche or corner can inject a little mystery into the most spartan cube of a room, suggesting the possibility of a shadowy corridor or hidden doorway beyond. By giving the illusion of greater depth, an artful bit of drapery can make a small space like a studio apartment look larger.

There are a number of ways to use curtains as dividers, but I prefer the easiest and least expensive method in the world: two screw eyes and a sturdy string, cord, or rope. Unlike a rod, it will bow in the middle—a look I happen to like. If you have a low ceiling or are covering a long expanse—say 15 feet or more—you will probably want to put a long drywall screw into your ceiling midway across, and wire it on at the same height (or higher) as the hooks on each side.

If you prefer, of course, you can also mount a café or pole-type rod on the ceiling—thick wooden rods that won't bow are best. (A bowed cord and a bowed rod are not the same thing!) Hang the drape from wooden, iron, or tarnished brass rings, or use tab-top drapes. If you want something really sumptuous and don't care if you can't draw it from one side to the other, try a one-sided swag. If you want to let light through, choose a semi-sheer fabric or one with an open weave. Remember that the curtain needs to look good from both sides, so either choose a fabric that doesn't have a wrong side, or buy enough to double it back-to-back.

The shelf at left is just a board screwed into the wall, with a curtain valance thumbtacked around the edges. The wall behind the bed on page 56 is painted brick; the other three walls (all unpainted drywall) have been covered with canvas drop cloths, which were "aged" by taking them out to the country and soaking them in a creek! A battered tin teapot, folding camp chair, wooden trunk, and clothes stored in burlap bags complete the outback effect.

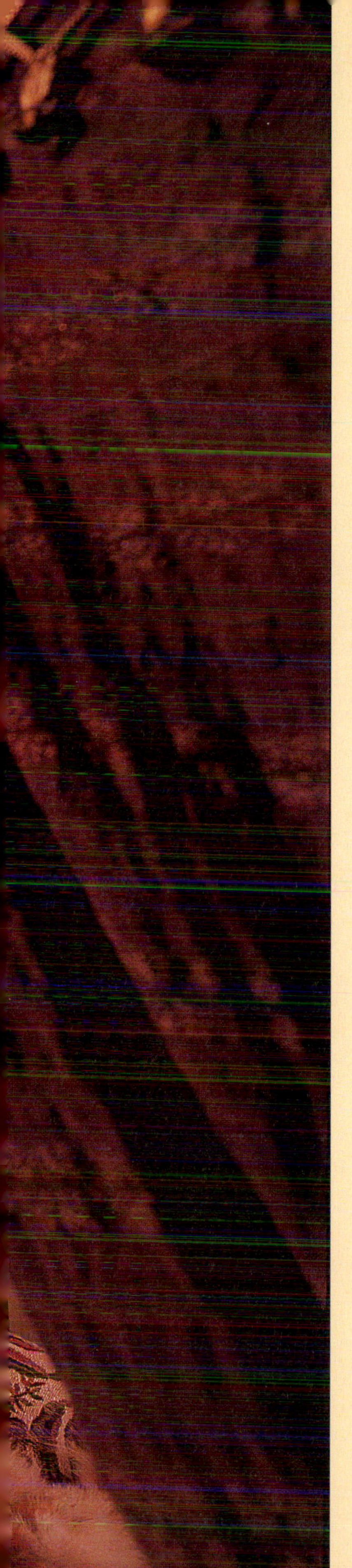

[Four: *Exotic*]

Pages 62–63
This niche would never feel so cozy if it weren't lit. In here, candles and incense would be a bit claustrophobic, not to mention dangerous, but a couple of tiny lamps give it just the right warm glow. Daybed bolsters and cushions line the back and sides; above them, narrow shelves are bracketed to the walls and hold collectibles as well as materials for reading, writing, and sketching. Curling up in here with a good book and a cup of tea is like taking a vacation in your own living room.

Right: Sectioned off from the rest of the living area by a curtain, this "studio" is only about 5 by 5 feet. It's a good example of how you can carve a comfortable work space out of one corner of a room. Messier art supplies are hidden behind the fabric panel tacked along the counter; other items are simply tacked up or stored in a utilitarian way, with no real thought to making the arrangement look good—yet it's very attractive. In fact, this little corner, like the studio in Chapter Six, "Alienated," is a favorite spot for many visitors. Perhaps it's because both are slightly unruly, without fixed boundaries—like thought in process. It says things are going on here, *and that's very appealing.*

If natural history is the animus that enlivens the rooms in Expedition, Eros is the anima that presides in Exotic. Here a series of drab rooms in a big prewar apartment building has been turned into something as sensual and comfortably decadent as a private car on the Orient Express. The bed-sitting room is especially luxurious with its spinet piano, comfortable sofa and chairs, and grand bed. It's like a Victorian gentleman's private retreat—the sort of salon that Sherlock Holmes would have appreciated, or Lord Byron before him. Even the closet harbors secret luxuries.

Unlike Spare and Expedition, where the nature of the collection itself generates the overall design scheme, this is a case where the collecting is almost completely in the service of creating a particular ambience. Bryan Purcell is a visual artist who happens to love old bars and gaudy strip joints, and his home is characterized by a similar atmosphere: the lighting muted but brilliantly warm, the decor fanciful and a tad libidinous. Its primary component is intoxicating color—carried out in yards and yards of richly colored fabric. Serious attitude and DIY art, almost everything else is a grand illusion created out of cast-off furniture, some lumber and a few hand tools, and the sorts of decorative objects (paper lanterns and beads and brass) that you find for lunch money in Chinatown and at hole-in-the-wall India import stores.

Like many interiors in this book, and more so than most, Bryan's apartment is hooshed like a theater set; if he moved, most of his impressive effects would break down into components and you'd never know, looking at the contents of the moving van, what his home would look like. Bryan has a certain painterly knack for trompe l'oeil, and he's created some impressive-looking pieces of furniture out of curbside finds and components from the local junk shop. It's not all smoke and mirrors—it was a little more laborious than that—but see that grand poster bed with the canopy? No posts. The inviting alcove divan? No alcove. And the interesting cupboards and armoires are fashioned from bits of shelving, remnants, paintings . . .

What holds it all together is color—a rich, saturated, offbeat palette that breaks all the usual rules. The ceilings throughout are painted a deep, plummy brown; much of the woodwork is flat black. In the hall, deep gray walls are trimmed with green. It's a scheme inspired by the stand of peacock feathers in the bed-sitting-room, and as somber as it sounds, the effect is warm and opulent.

The first thing you lay eyes on in the foyer is one of Bryan's paintings—a nude that looks sort of old, sort of new, and pays homage to figures from Ingres and Manet. In his work, he deliberately tries to incorporate both traditional and modern elements, so that it spans the decades. A Victorian sofa and a Casbah curtain of peacock blue beads further set the tone. So do scent and sound: the minute you walk into his house you're enveloped by scent, and nearly every door you walk through is hung with small, inconspicuous bells—tiny chimes that go off whenever you brush against them. Sound and scent can be as important to setting the tone as a beautiful candelabrum, and this entrance is a case in point. Attention to the *total* atmosphere makes it a prime example of the second rule of display: whatever you see (and experience) first should be important. Everything about this foyer lets you know you're in someplace different, special, sexy.

Exotic amply demonstrates how far you can go with what you can afford and what you've already got. Without waiting around until he could get exactly the "right" pieces for each room, Bryan set out to re-create his total environment—and he did it on a shoestring. This exotic cocoon was created largely out of oddments, in a series of slightly battered apartment-house rooms that had one big thing going for them: 9½-foot ceilings.

The focal point in the living room is an alcove bed that looks like something out of the Arabian Nights; it's no more than a loft bed, but it's far more attractive in costume, with the lower level fitted out for comfort. The coffee table is laid out with a mismatched green tea set decorated with silver dragons; eating from these turns Chinese takeout into something adventurous. In the salon-style bedroom, the canopy bed is faked with three one-by-twelves, some molding, paint, and draperies; all the seating is secondhand. One chair is a find from the street reupholstered with fake fur! Bryan took apart the original cover and used it as a pattern, then attached the new fabric with a staple gun, using braid trim and hot glue to cover the raw edges.

In many ways, both the attitude and the scheme itself are retro 1960s, but reinvented. Bryan has always been drawn to things Turkish and generally Eastern, and with so many sources for inexpensive Asian imports around the country, it's an absolutely great mode for decorating on a budget. The trick is to integrate inexpensive new objects with genuinely old things. Add the enticement of incense and candlelight, and you get the exotic feel of an Edwardian-era opium den, without the menace.

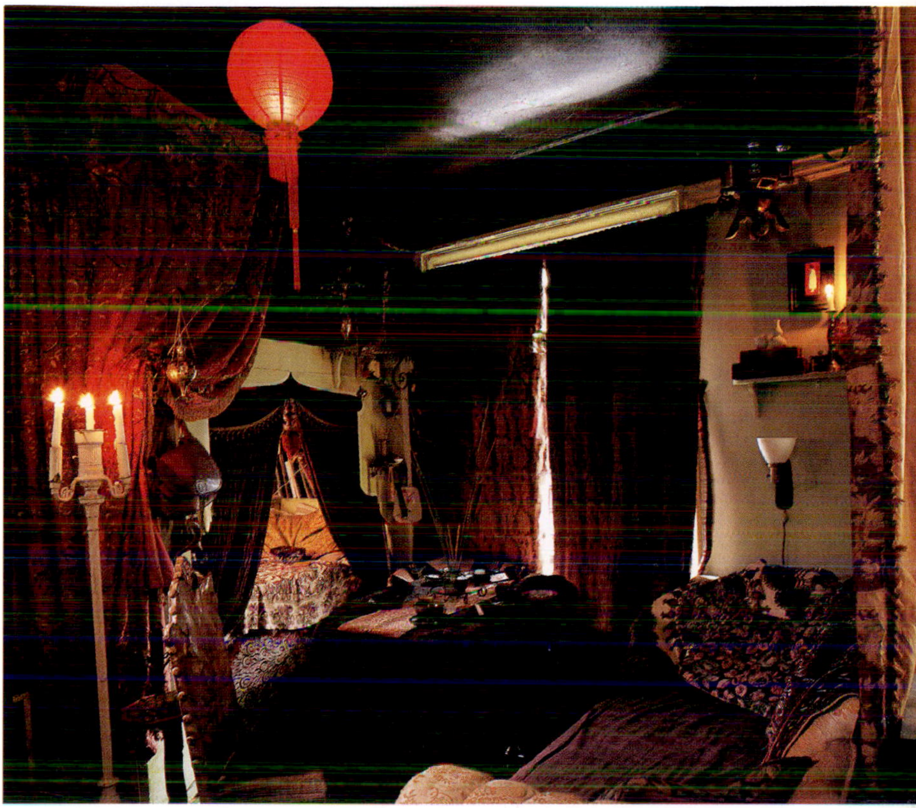

The alcove divan is essentially the same construction as a loft bed, with a mattress on the upper platform and curvy front panels cut from pine. The coffee table is an old oval table covered with dyed jacquard. Another vintage floor-lamp-cum-candelabrum, plus single candlesticks practically everywhere, create a warm glow at night. Folding fans, brass bells, incense burners, and paper lanterns decorated with extra fringe add to the feeling that you're around the corner from an exotic street bazaar in Morocco or Hong Kong.

Keys to Exotic

Visit some night spots. Darkly lit but with jolts of color, vintage saloons, burlesque shows, and unrestored turn-of-the-century bars (like the Old Town in Manhattan) have the kind of somber but sexy atmosphere you see in Exotic. Scope out whatever is available in your town. If you'd rather stay home, rent some old Basil Rathbone movies as well as films like *Cabaret*, *Gaslight*, *Murder on the Orient Express*, and anything set in the Casbah.

Sink your money into good fabrics. And if you possibly can, get your hands on some fabulous old secondhand draperies. Combine these with less expensive fabrics in rich, earthy tones—dye them if you need to—and be very generous with the yardage.

Visit import stores. If there's no Chinatown in your city, you can find inexpensive Chinese and Indian imports at places like Pier One as well as at small import stores in malls all over the country. This is a way to get a lot of hoosh stuff for not much money.

Avoid obvious 1960s clichés. Even though this look revisits the 1960s in some ways, it's a very different feel. Unless you plan to open a head shop, at all costs avoid tie dyes, India-import bedspreads, batiks, cheap incense, eucalyptus, pampas grass, and all those awful dried-and-dyed weeds you find in craft stores. And please, *no wicker*!

Who'd have thought of putting a piano at the foot of a bed? This is the sort of striking effect you can get when you aren't afraid to push the furniture around and try unusual combinations. The grand canopy bed is an illusion created from little more than plain lumber and lots of fabric (see "Guerrilla Architecture," page 71). A small light mounted at its head has a long tassel pull, so that you can turn the light on and off without getting up. More luxury is at hand in a chair that's been reupholstered with fake fur—a witty alternative to velvet.

Creating an Exotic Atmosphere

Exotic is a kind of sensual cocoon that includes all sorts of factors. It's a scheme designed to create a full-blown effect out of little more than flotsam, jetsam, and sleight of hand. Like the seven veils, soft fabrics are key to its illusions—but scent, sound, and a carefully considered color palette all play major roles in creating the total atmosphere.

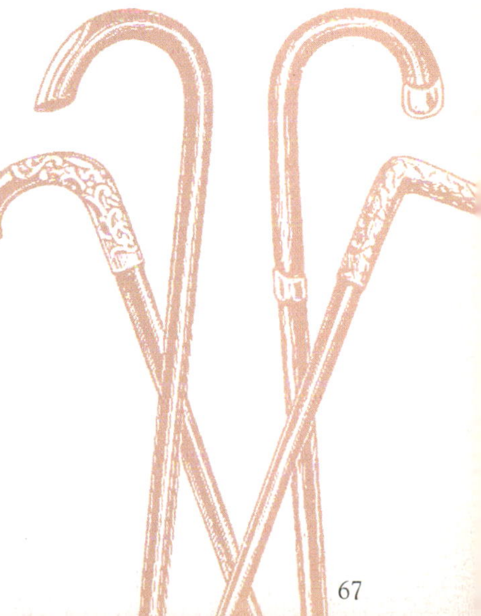

Above and right: Walls, furniture, and draperies in the bedroom are done in shades of rich plum brown and black—all except for one brilliant niche, which is actually a closet fitted out in an intense Chinese red. Built-in shelves are covered and draped with fabric and matching red fringe, and the space is crowded with portraits, mirrors, colorful shawls, red silk Chinese lanterns, and memorabilia. To the right of the closet, an armoire effect is created out of a set of open shelves painted black and topped by a framed picture that actually hangs from the ceiling. On the left side, another set of open shelves is masked by fabric panels and mounted over a small writing table—a construction that mimics an old-fashioned secretary.

Choosing a Palette

So much depends on the powerful element of color. It can soothe the senses; it can simplify, blend, and enhance a decor. Picking a palette is the first and perhaps most essential thing to do when you're creating your home environment.

Start by selecting a group of colors that you're drawn to. You could argue that all colors are fabulous—why be limited to a few? I don't agree. You need to be passionate about a color scheme, not indecisive. That doesn't necessarily mean all your colors "match." Plum brown, black, gray, green, and peacock blue (plus a single zap of scarlet) don't match in most people's books, but in Exotic, they work.

Whatever your favorite colors are, write them down and then pick out an example of each from chips at the paint store. Go home and cut each favorite out (you don't want to confuse yourself with other shades on the strip) and then see how they react with one another. Do they feel good to you? Pull out any that don't. You're not going to be able to find everything in these exact shades, of course, but it will help if you staple the chips together on a sheet and keep them in your wallet so you can at least have a guide. If you have a really hard time choosing from your favorite twenty-five hues, try picking a different palette for each room.

When you do make your choices, stay with them; you will grow to love them the more you use them. There is no such thing as the "right" color, so you can't choose wrong.

Picking a palette helps tremendously in shopping. It creates answers like "Wrong color—and too big to repaint. Skip it" and "Right *exact* shade of green and I don't have any yet—buy it now!" Or "Do I need this velvet? Yes—I'm not going to get that saturated red out of a can of paint."

You get the idea. It's simple enough—but honestly, failing to select a palette is one of the biggest mistakes I see people make in their homes. Look at Spare, Expedition, and Exotic: each has a palette, however subtle; each is distinctly different; and each interior would completely change character if you switched the three palettes around. That's the power of color!

Furniture in Drag

The old "front parlor" idea still seems to be alive and well in many homes, where the owners have sunk all their money into a few fancy furnishings for the living room, and only next of kin are allowed in the comfortable eyesore called the "family room." Nor would the family ever hang out in the "living room" if it weren't for the occasional guest.

If this book is about anything, it's about the importance of being comfortable in your home, in an environment that pleases all your senses, visual and otherwise. Don't go without necessary furnishings just because you can't find or afford exactly the right, beautiful piece. If you really need a chair or chest and stumble across something really cheap—or better yet, free—go for it. Take it home, fix it up, make it fit. If you paid $2 for it, what have you lost when the time comes to throw it out? A few years down the road, you may even discover it has turned into a collectible antique in your care.

The furniture in Exotic is strong evidence: even if you can't make a silk purse out of a sow's ear, you can turn out a good imitation.

Do you have a battered cupboard or desk and a mismatched set of shelves about the same width? Stack them or screw one piece into the wall and center the other below it. Paint them to match or coordinate, hang a panel of beautiful fabric over the shelves, and you'll have something that has the effect of an armoire or old-fashioned secretary.

Are you stuck with one of those hideous loft beds made to save space in a small apartment? Turn it into an alcove with some lumber, paint, and more fabric. Do you sleep on an unornamented Hollywood bed—you know, box springs, mattress, bare metal frame with casters? Buy some lumber, paint, and *lots* of fabric, and create an elegant canopy that's attached to the ceiling instead of the bed itself.

Draping fabric all over everything may not be the way to go in all situations, but in Exotic it's just right for the mood and a great way to transform cosmetically challenged furnishings. Call it furniture in drag. Call it guerrilla architecture. In the Exotic decor shown here, all of these effects were constructed with a needle, thread, and hand tools. If you have a few basic power tools and a sewing machine, so much the better.

Guerrilla Architecture

The first commandment of hooshing is *If you can't see it, don't muck with it.* Guerrilla architecture works on the principle of creating great visual effects as if you were making theater props—coaxing them out of disparate components and ignoring all those niceties only a certified architect or cabinetmaker would notice. Below are tips on making a canopy, disguising a loft bed, and transforming a closet. (See page 68 for ideas on faking an armoire or secretary.) These don't include plans or woodworking instructions, which are beyond the scope of this book—but none of the projects requires much more than a basic familiarity with a hammer, saw, screwdriver, and measuring tape.

A Canopy Bed The grand canopy over the bed shown on page 65 is simply a wooden frame cut to size from one-by-twelves, painted matte black, and fastened to the ceiling with corner brackets (drive the screws into the ceiling joists, which are normally 16 inches apart, like the studs in the walls). If you want the draperies to have a straight drop, the frame should be as long and wide as your bed; make it a couple of inches smaller both ways if you want the drapes to curve out over the bed's corners.

Plain square wood molding painted to match was glued to the upper edge of the boards, to give the frame a more finished appearance. Square molding looks all right even if you don't miter it; use fancier molding if you wish, but it has to be mitered. Hang the draperies from curtain rods bracketed to the lower inside edge of the frame (don't forget they need to go around the corners) or use upholstery tacks to fasten the fabric directly to the wood.

If you're lucky enough to have a foyer, this is the place to set the tone of your whole house. The plastic peacock-blue beads in the doorway may look tacky in the store, but against the green and gray walls they complete the palette and suit the setting. In addition to the large painting—a major AGM (attention-getting mechanism)—another standout in this foyer is the standing candelabrum. This one is made from an old floor lamp with the cord chopped off and candles stuck in. Both the old lamp and the plastic beads demonstrate that if a piece fits in and helps set a mood, it doesn't matter if it isn't beautiful in itself.

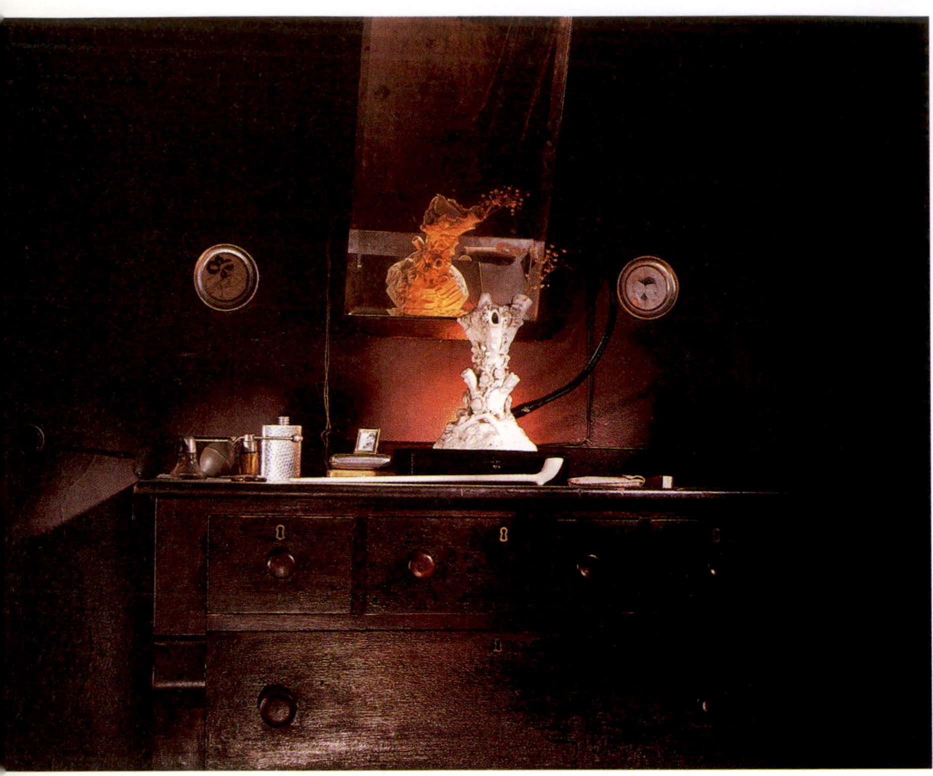

Here are an old broken white vase, a few mementos, and some necessities, all highlighted by a pearly glow from a tiny lamp created from an armature, a bulb, and a small panel of fringed fabric.

An Alcove Bed Breaking the usual rules, the alcove bed in the living room is snugged up into a corner, so that only one end of the structure needed to be enclosed (if you use plywood for this, it should be at least 3/4 inch thick). The inside surface of the end panel was painted to match the walls; although the outside surface is concealed by drapery, paint it too to discourage warping. The curvy front panels are simply one-by-twelve pine, cut, in this case, with a handsaw; use a power jigsaw and the job will go faster. The wood was then sanded, painted, and waxed. If you use plywood instead of pine for the front panels, you'll need to work on the cut edges, either filling and sanding them until you get a smooth finish or covering them with veneer, which can be bought in rolls at lumber supply stores.

A Closet Hoosh Take an ordinary closet and turn it into something dramatic in a few simple steps. Start by removing the clothes bar, if it has one, then cover the walls with fabric or wallpaper and add shelves covered in material to match or coordinate. If you want a concealed storage space, curtain off the top couple of shelves or hang a fabric skirt from a lower shelf to the floor. Add moldings, braid, fringe, or other trims, if you wish, then hoosh the open shelves with collectibles, barware, pictures—whatever you like. A single waist-high shelf would be a dramatic place to exhibit a large sculpture, vitrine, or your favorite mementos. To get the biggest impact out of it, be sure to add lighting. A single overhead light will leave the lower shelves in darkness, so either put a small lamp on each shelf, use light strips made especially for shelving, or hide your light sources along the inside of the door frame. Leave the door on so that the exhibit can be closed, or remove both door and hinges for a niche effect.

Scent, Sound, and Other Aspects of Hooshing

Hooshing can go beyond the realm of the visual: take into account music, fragrance, and even what *you* look like in your house. Bryan Purcell has a fabulous handle on this aspect. When you walk into his apartment, you're at once met with various stimuli that catapult you immediately into his domain. He greets you in a full black silk Chinese pajama ensemble and velvet Chinese slippers, his hair twisted with chopsticks. You hear soul music and smell a faint waft of incense that grows stronger as you enter each room. The fragrance differs depending upon the time of day, because Bryan has been working on the use of trigger-based scent as a means to induce certain moods. For instance, he lights a specific incense whenever he is relaxed, building the association until that scent can be used to actually trigger a sense of relaxation.

This is a fairly complex concept, so I won't go any further, other than to say don't forget your sense of smell. It can be a powerful mood-inducing element in a hoosh, and with so many new, mild incenses and home fragrances on the market, it's an element worth playing with.

I don't take it as far as Bryan does, but I do use a scented candle that's very effective: Banana Republic makes one called "Green Vine." I light it when I clean my house—it smells very fresh and lingers wonderfully in fabrics. Crabtree & Evelyn makes a nice vanilla spray that I spritz between my bedsheets. I don't have a fireplace, so at Christmas I burn bits of pine, Christmas tree needles, and myrrh on charcoal disks (you find them wherever you find incense) to evoke the scent. And when I want to recall an incredible trip to the canyon lands, I light a small twig of juniper that came from the desert, then close my eyes and remember a juniper wood fire on a starry night.

I suggest staying away from floral scents and any of those fragrances that pervade malls and craft shops. Buy from a good store that specializes in all varieties, rather than from the grocery store or the local head shop. Go for unusual scents based on natural essences of citrus or wood, or single scents like amber and heather (not lavender—we've had enough!). Even if you buy a relatively expensive home fragrance, you're not going to be investing much—generally the range is between $5 and $15. There are also incredible incense bargains in Chinatown, and the packaging is amazing.

Have fun finding incense *burners*, too. I put stick incense into a dried-out lime, cone incense in one of those round glass cups once used to keep chair legs from making holes in the wall-to-wall. You find them at junk stores all the time—they look like thick, undersized petri

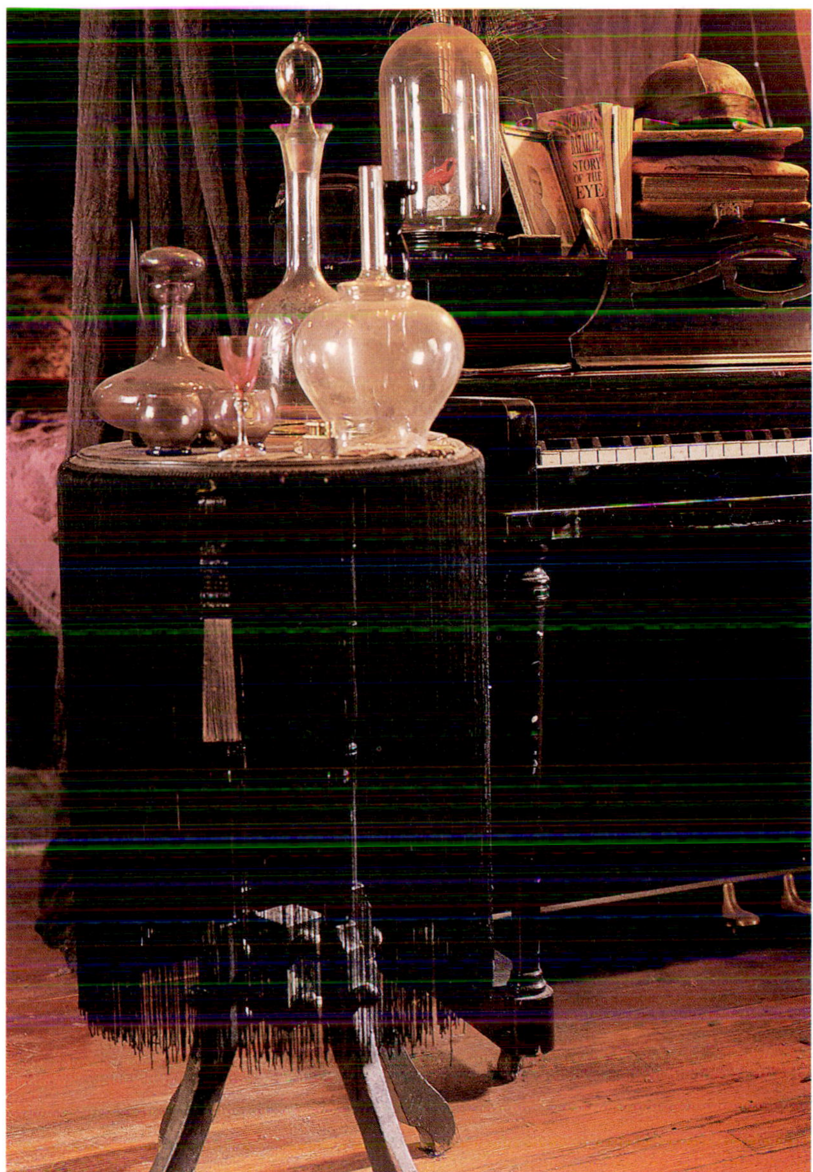

This common side table or fern stand has been made uncommon by adding long, black trim fringe to its edge.

One smashing, authentic piece can do wonders for a hoosh—especially if you're largely faking it. In this case it's a fabulous old Asian drape of red embroidery that wraps an outer corner of the bed's upper frame. The curtains in the front opening are made from two more panels of inexpensive jacquard, dyed to coordinate with the palette, trimmed with fringe, and finished off with a big, elegant tassel to complete the Arabian Nights sedan chair effect. Large tassels like this are usually pricy: This one is handmade, using a wooden finial and fringe trim from the fabric store (see instructions on page 79).

dishes and they're great for incense. If you want, you can put a glass light cover over the dish and watch the smoke come out of the top hole; you'll probably need several cones to create a good effect. Old standing metal ashtrays are also great for incense burners.

Hooshing with Sound

We all have our driving-down-the-highway tapes, our own versions of Barry White/cozy-sexy CDs, our hot party tunes and favorite oldies. But don't stop with these; keep going. What about rainy Sunday morning music? (I recommend the soundtrack from *Room with a View.*) Or medieval dinner music? (The Cloisters Museum has tons.) Then there's music to make dinner by (Neil Young, *After the Gold Rush*). One of my favorite things to do when cruising junk stores and bad yard sales is to buy scratchy, corny old 1950s albums. The covers are fabulous, the titles hilarious, and the prices range from 10¢ to $1. Nothing is better for a cocktail party or for eating Chinese takeout than these old albums: not knowing who the artist is or what the album is going to sound like adds to the fun—you'll laugh, you'll dance, you'll cry! If you don't have a phonograph any longer, buy one cheap at a yard sale or get an old 45 player in a carrying case, like you had as a kid.

I am also a staunch believer in *looking like* you live in your house. If you have an incredibly cozy country home, don't show up at the door in leggings and a big white shirt. Cruise the vintage stores, buy an appropriate old petticoat and an oversized sweater. I guarantee they are as comfortable. Richard Dayne, whose apartment looks medieval (see Chapter Seven, "Alchemy"), always wears some outfit that reminds you of a scene from *Excalibur*. If nothing else, buy a robe and slippers that are in tune with your setting. *You* are more a part of your environment than the ideal chair—even if no one is there to see you. I think we all know the power of dressing to make us believe in who we are. If you're into the power suit, how about the power of a brocade robe and leather slippers! Or better yet, escape the power suit and put on lace and cashmere to wear around your house, so that you find some balance and softness after the corporate part of your day. If you look good, you feel better. No one looks good in sweatpants and a decal T-shirt. They are for jogging. And I don't want to hear that dumb "comfortable" story. Nothing is more comfortable than a dress—and I mean for men, too (Bryan often wears a long gauze one around the house).

The point is, it's your house, so wear something mood-setting and sensual. Allow yourself to *escape* from your outside life. You might just find yourself drinking less and watching less TV.

TASSELS

People tend to love tassels or hate 'em. If you love them, you've probably already discovered how expensive they are. Even at discount craft stores a sizable tassel can run $25 or more. And you rarely need just one.

Making your own really isn't that hard. They won't look like the kind you buy, but they'll get the point across—and personally I prefer something less stuffy than ready-made tassels, which tend to be too glossy and fancy.

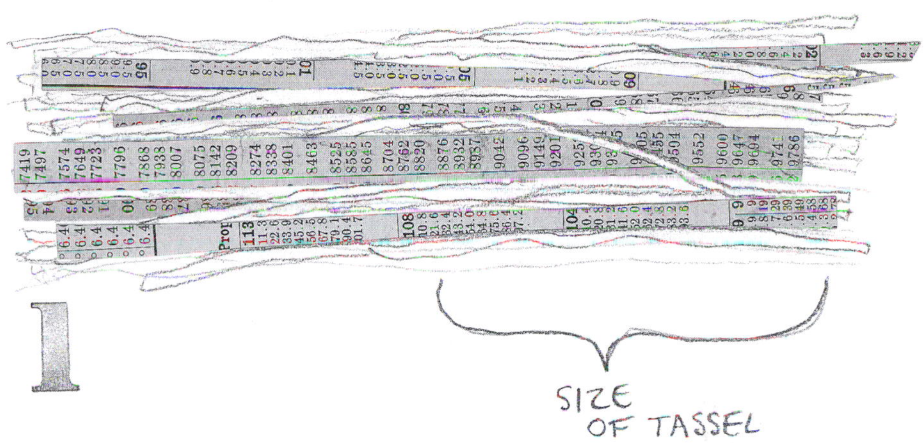

SOFT TASSELS

To make a small, soft tassel, the kind you'd put on a pillow, on the corners of a throw, or in the center of a valance, you'll need several yards of ribbonlike material. Most tassels are made with acetate or cotton string, but you don't have to stick to that. Here are some ideas: rayon seam binding (cheap!), sequin trim, satin ribbon, soutache braid, narrow grosgrain, embroidery thread, yarn, raffia, natural twine, soft cotton string (all thicknesses), and leftover gift wrap ribbon. I like to combine two or three different materials: I made one set with sequin trim, seam binding, and string, and even tied a couple of little shoe buttons to the ends of some of the longer strands. Pick a combination that appeals to you. I'd use color as a guide.

Now, sometimes it's hard to decide what size you want, but the longer and thicker you want the tassel, the more material you'll need. Keep in mind that the thinner the strands, the more yards it will take. If you're using string or embroidery thread, you'll need more yards than if you use a wider ribbon, and it will take a bit longer to make. (If the first one you make doesn't turn out the way you want, use it on a package instead of a bow.)

Step 1: Cut the strands into lengths that are a little more than twice as long as you want the finished tassel. Lay the strands in a neat pile as you cut, so that you can get an idea of how thick the tassel will be—remembering that the finished tassel

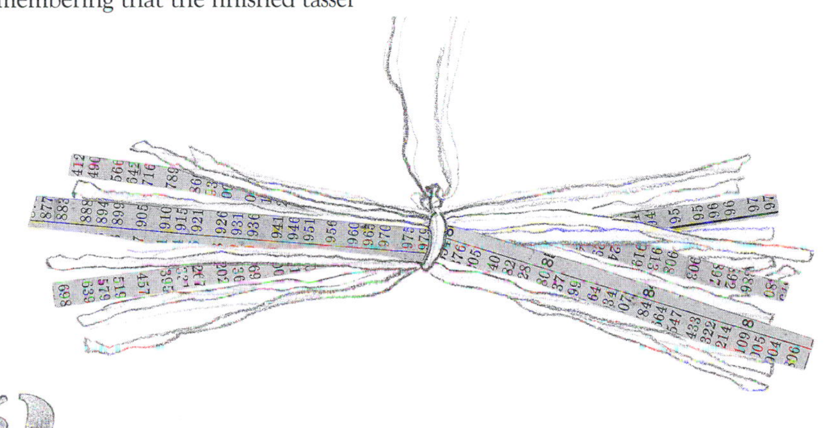

Step 2: Cut an extra length and tie it around the bundle at the exact midpoint, making a tight double knot and leaving the ends hanging out.

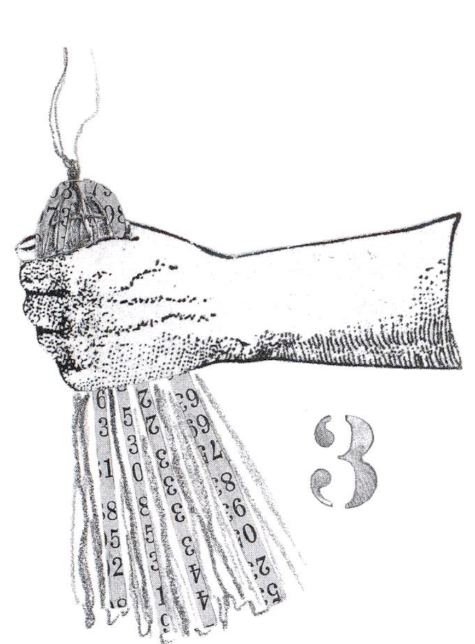

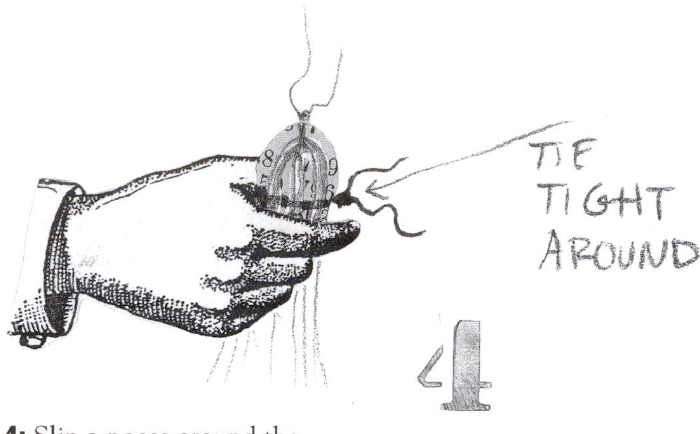

Step 4: Slip a noose around the top, tie it as tightly as you can (easier if you have someone to help), and double-knot it.

Step 3: Grasp the tassel by the loose ends of the knot and pull the doubled strands through your other fist until just the top, folded part protrudes. Depending upon how long the finished tassel is, the top should be from 3/4 inch to 2 inches long; on a small tassel, this could be one-third of the total length.

Step 5: Now you have a tassel! You can trim the ends evenly if you wish, but leaving them scrappy is nice. Finish it off by dipping into water or into coffee if you want to age it and blend the colors. Squeeze and shake it out and hang to dry.

An alternate method: Wind your string or ribbon (not too tight) around a square of stiff cardboard cut to the size you want your tassel. Slip a strand under the loops along the top edge, and tie tightly with a double knot. Then snip the loops straight across the bottom edge, and proceed with step 3.

FINIAL TASSELS

Tassels like Bryan's, with the wooden top, are just as easy. For these you'll need either a painted wooden finial, old or new, or a wooden tassel top which looks like a cap with a hole through it (you'll need to paint these too). They are sold in trim shops—in Manhattan I found some in the trim district on 38th Street, between Fifth Avenue and Broadway.

Next you'll need several yards of fringe trim. The length of the fringe will be the length of the tassel, so buy long fringe if your wooden top is big.

Last, you'll need a hot-glue gun.

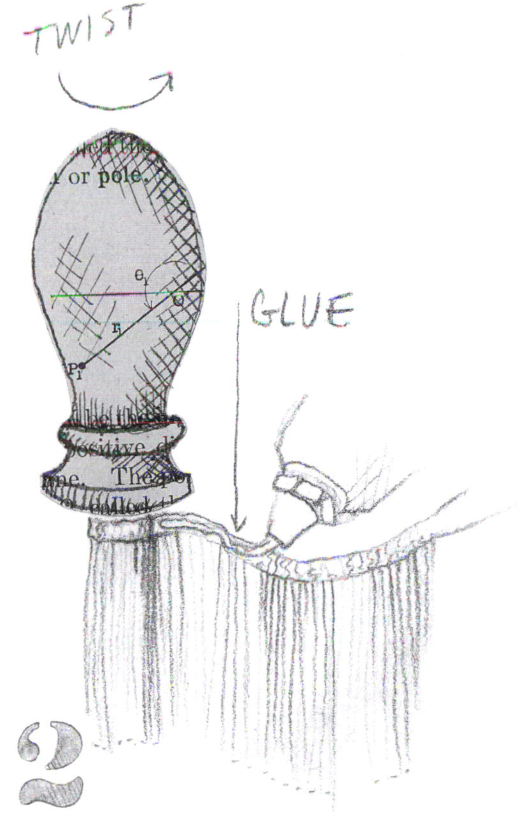

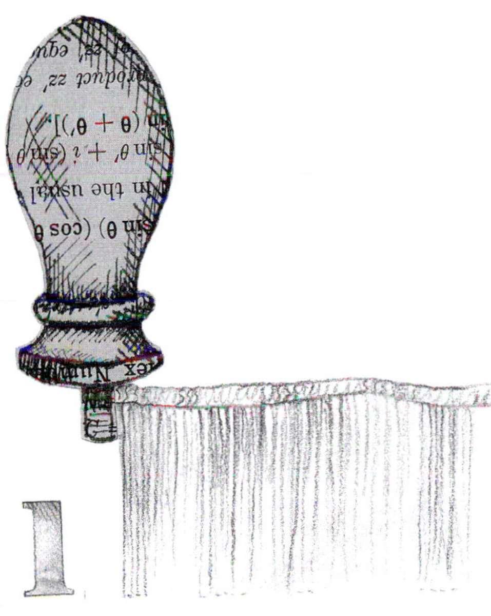

Step 1: Take the finial and glue one end of the strip of fringe to the finial post, flush against the base of the finial.

Step 2: Now continue by applying a thin bead of glue, about 1 inch long, along the inside edge of the strip. Using the finial as a handle, twist it so that the glued edge winds evenly around the post. Keep the edge flush against the base of the finial as you go, and apply glue only an inch or so at a time so that it doesn't harden before you get the edge adhered. Continue gluing and winding until the fringe is *almost* as big around as the finial, then stop, snip off the excess, and apply a final dab of hot glue to the end.

Remember not to touch the hot glue with your bare finger. If you need to dab it down, lick your finger first and be quick—otherwise the glue will stick and burn your skin.

Step 3: Put a small screw-eye in the finished tassel for hanging.

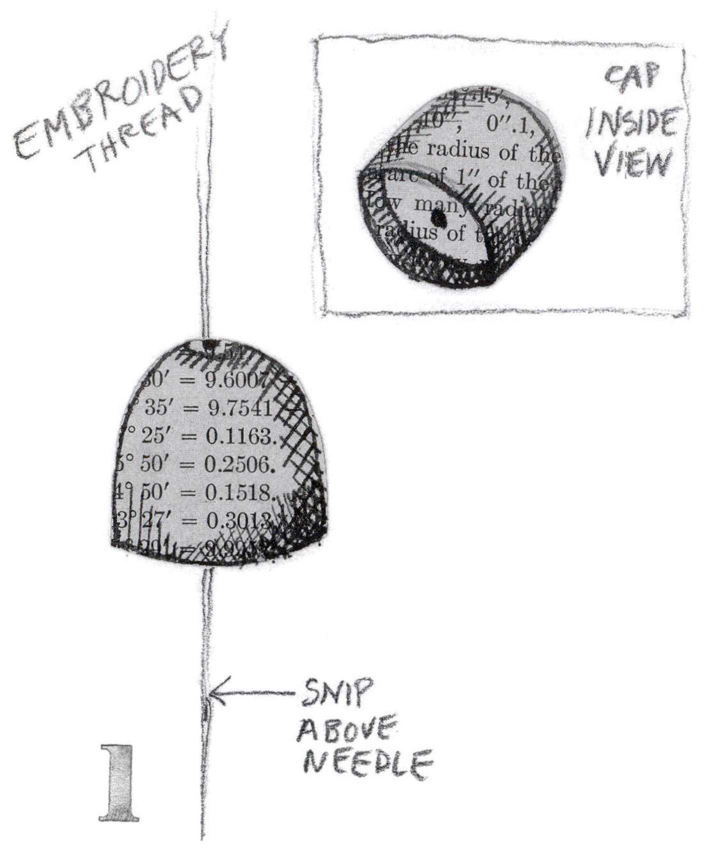

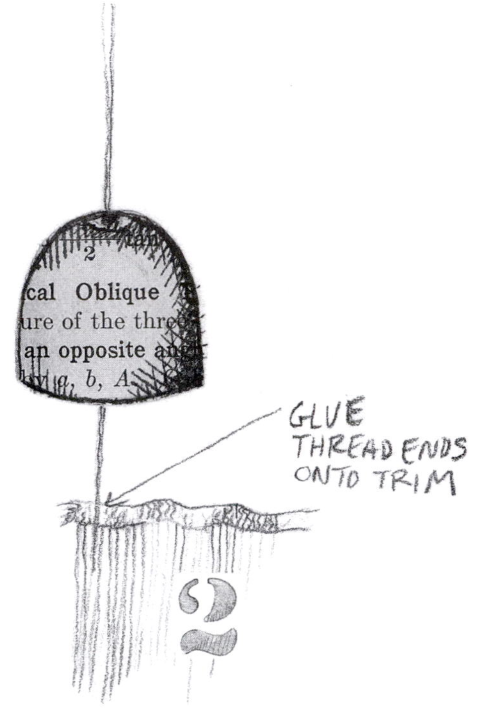

WOOD-TOP TASSELS

You can buy ready-made wooden tassel tops at many places that sell upholstery and drapery fabrics. Because they're made for the purpose, these are even easier.

Step 1: Put a loop of embroidery thread or string through the hole so that the loop extends a few inches below the open, cup-shaped part of the cap. (You can use a big darning needle for this.) Then proceed in one of two ways:

Snip your ribbon or string into lengths according to the directions for the small soft tassel on page 77. Insert the bundle halfway through the loop you've made in the cap. Make sure the strands are centered, then pull up on the ends of the loop, drawing the strands up into the cap. Tie a tight double knot as close to the upper hole as you can, to keep the tassel from pulling out. If the top opening is large, you may need to thread the loop ends through a small wooden or glass bead before tying them off.

Step 2: Or use fringe trim again. Make sure the loop is long enough to resist pulling out. Now apply a dab of glue to one end of the fringe trim and lay the loop in it.

Step 3: After it's set a moment, carefully roll the fringe around itself just enough to give you a base.

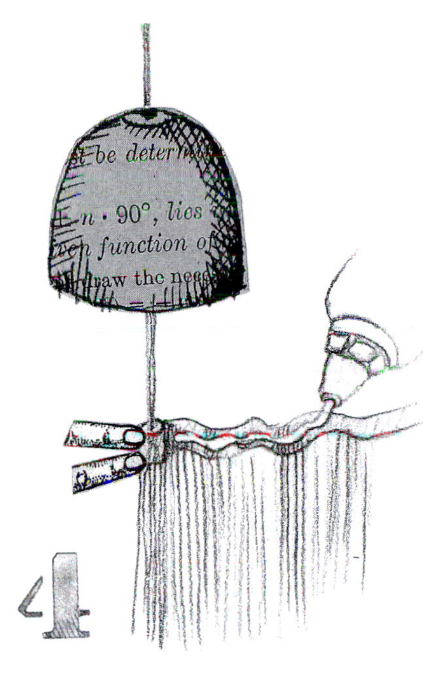

Step 4: Then apply hot glue to the inside edge of the trim, about an inch at a time, and wind the fringe around itself as described with the finial.

Step 5: Stop and trim off when the roll is as big around as the inside of the cap, then pull through, and voilà!

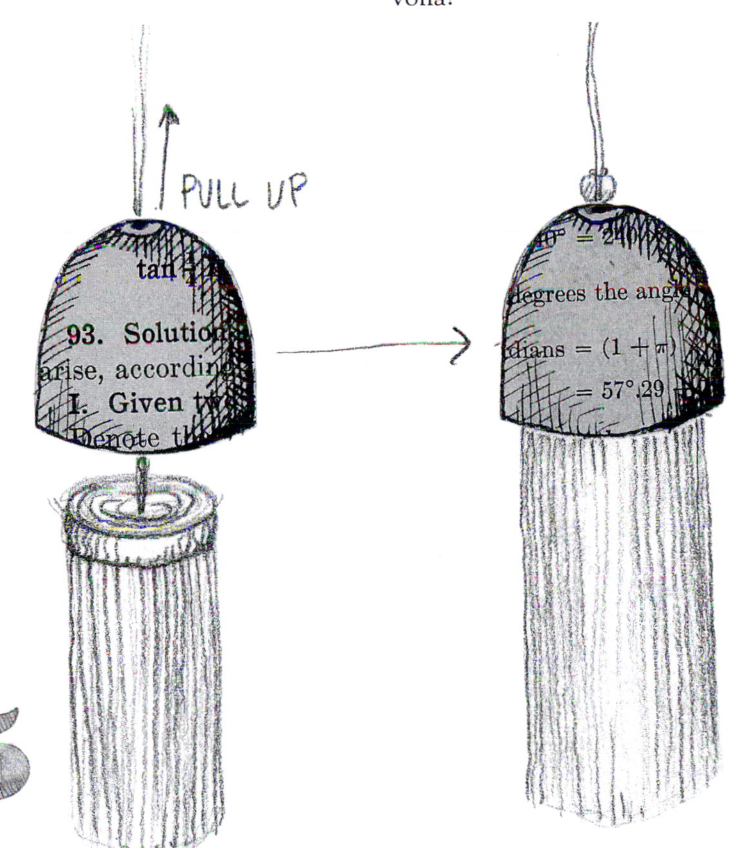

[Five: ***Humble***]

Pages 82–83
Separate areas—We see the eating/observing area on the left by the window; the sleeping/resting area in the right far corner; the sewing/reading area to the right in front.

This afternoon "folly" had the humblest of beginnings: a little tumbledown outbuilding that was once used as a henhouse. Beavers had toppled one of the trees outside—nature taking a hand in letting in more light.

Right: The window is a prime spot for bird-watching, so a birding book and a pair of old opera glasses are appropriate props. The locale was one of several cues that made birds and sewing an obvious choice for the dominant themes, and there are scores of collectibles available that fit both. A robin-redbreast pincushion, a pair of needlepoint birds, button collections, and an artificial goldfinch to place in a home-made birdcage were found at local flea markets. The wire mesh cover over the slice of cake was made to keep insects off food; an old-fashioned outfitted picnic basket would also be right at home on this table.

The interior pictured here is a totally impromptu hoosh that Morgan Puett and I put together in an old henhouse on the grounds of a turn-of-the-century farm. We think of it as an "afternoon folly," with a Depression-era look. It's a sort of summer retreat in a tumbledown space furnished entirely with items either borrowed from home or bought from a local outlet that sells auction leftovers. We set two limits on ourselves: we had to do this on the cheap, and quickly. In the daytime the folly is a great place to read, have a cup of tea, watch birds—or just escape the summer guests up at the big house.

The principles we followed apply to hooshing any tiny space. Although the room comes together in a pleasing whole, the arrangement of furnishings suggests distinctly different areas for working, napping, or just looking out the window—and each is approached as if it were a separate still life.

As a concept, Humble encapsulates the sorts of old-fashioned, homely pastimes of an era before TV and the Internet: bird-watching, reading, mending. There's no plumbing or wiring in our folly, but there's plenty of natural light, and in the evening the space is beautifully lit by candles.

Its dilapidated state set the tone: The walls are beautifully stained from the leaky roof, which at one point was partly covered with heavy plastic to keep the rain out. The big hole over the cot was a bonus—a skylight! Like other proper summer houses, this rustic version largely ignores the usual boundaries between "indoors" and "outdoors." The floor inside is cement that is cracked and broken in places—it's cement and dirt, actually. In fact there was so much dirt in one corner of the shed that Morgan just decided to make a garden out of it! She planted raspberry and sweet pea and a couple of interesting weeds there—and enough light enters the shed to keep the plants alive. Eventually she plans to put in some herbs.

Like the garden, another major element in our decorating scheme—birds—came as a gift. You can barely see some trailing bits in the photograph, but above the small lace-draped window (page 82) is a bird's nest. It belonged to a little house wren that charmed us by flying in and out of the shack while we were doing our own nesting.

What could be more appropriate for an old henhouse than a bird theme? Man-made bird images are easy to come by, too. One of those wire-and-feather birds you find at craft stores and at Christmas is right at home perched in a neat homemade birdcage we hung from the ceiling; we found a pair of framed needlepoints depicting birds to hang on the wall below it. Birds are the theme; sewing, the subtheme—the needlepoints and a terrific robin-red-breast pincushion made the connection.

Morgan has a pink-painted table that fits perfectly under one window; it looks out over a pasture, and is a great spot for watching real live birds. We put a pair of opera glasses close by for spotting rare species. The table hoosh includes a bird book and a notebook for recording our discoveries—so far about fifty different species from this one vantage point.

The daybed was put together from an old rusty cot frame we dragged out of a barn. We put a piece of foam rubber on it and covered it with fabric, adding an old quilt and a couple of pillows that we bought at a secondhand store.

Curtains and fabric—quilts, an old upholstered chair, rugs—do a lot to soften up this spartan little space. The 1940s floral rug under the table cost $15; other rugs were brought out from the house. At the windows I tacked up string and hung fabric over it. We found some inexpensive calico at the button store; I soaked it in a nearby creek to get it a little soiled-looking, then hung it up wet. This is a simple way to get a new piece of fabric to drape properly: hang it up wet and let it dry on the rod, so that the weight of the water pulls it into place. A piece of brand-new fabric with the bolt folds still showing would be totally out of place here. Our small calico panel looks like it's been hanging there since the Depression.

The bouquet consists of wildflowers we gathered between the house and shed. The old bucket and the various old tools around—the flyswatter handle among them—were either rescued from the barn or literally unearthed from the paddock and surrounding fields. Discovering things right under our noses was a big part of the fun in this adventure. When you return local artifacts, however humble, to a habitat like this, you feel you're reconstructing a little piece of history.

The garden/solarium is in the front left corner by the door.

Keys to Humble

Choose battered old objects with a handmade look to them. Humble is a style that allows you to go out and pick up all sorts of junky things that have an appealing shape or look. In the summer house pictured here, the emphasis is on worn but useful domestic goods: sewing implements, dishes, simple decorative objects.

Steer clear of cookie-cutter reproductions. Some new furnishings with battered finishes are okay; others look fake. Buy from secondhand stores whenever you can. You may be better off with an old unfinished ladderback chair from Sears than with an expensive new piece "distressed" by beatings with a chain, which approximates nothing you'd ever encounter outside a medieval dungeon.

Use a combination of fabrics. Faded linen and cotton prints will give you an authentic look; cartoon versions of calico (neon-bright color, bunnies and ducks, printed-on "quilting") will not. Nice reproduction prints can be stained with coffee or faded with heavy bleach.

Don't try to match anything. The items you select should be frowzily comfortable together, but *nothing* has to match. In fact, mismatches are often the best way to go for a rustic cottage look. If there's one unifying element, it's very subtle, faded color: here soft blues and faded pinks mix well with stained whites and natural wood tones.

Have fun! Collecting for a Humble scheme is like a scavenger hunt, full of surprises. For ideas or just to get into the mood, take a look at movies like *The Grapes of Wrath* and children's books like *The Boxcar Children* or *The Borrowers*.

Hooshing the Humble Interior

Characterized by simple, homemade furniture with battered paint, raw scrubbed floors, peeling wallpaper, and faded cottons and linens, Humble is essentially a Depression-era look, and the very antithesis of Exotic glamour. In my own private lexicon, I call it "spool." It's a

The seats of these two ladderbacks were replaced with linen torn into strips and woven over-and-under like the potholders kids make from jersey loops. The ends were simply knotted under the seat. Because recaning is so laborious, this rustic solution is simple, sturdy, and in keeping with the spirit of the place.

BREVITAS
WHITE OWL
REGENTS

This wooden structure on stilts is where the previous tenants—hens—actually laid their eggs. It makes an amusing bookcase.

disingenuous sensibility: decorative elements usually look naive and homemade, and many pieces are innocent of any decoration at all. Washed-out, sun-bleached colors are great in Humble, as are those small touches of straightforward primary color you find on enameled cookware and stone crockery. If your collections run toward domestic items like kitchenware, old buttons, and vintage quilts, Humble may be just the right setting. It's a great mode for antiques on the plain side—farmhouse cupboards, Hoosier cabinets, enameled metal tables, homemade shelving, wooden chairs with rush seating. And it's made to order for items that are so weathered and beat up, they're practically decrepit.

Quick Rehabilitations for Old Furniture The worn-and-scuffed look that's so appealing in real antiques isn't always what you find in pieces from the secondhand store, and it's often a temptation to put a lot of work into an old piece that doesn't have an appropriate patina. I know people who have bought a junk piece of furniture, stripped, restained, and waxed it, and got something that looked . . . okay, not great. And what a bother! Have you ever stripped paint? If not, don't torture yourself, and if you have, *don't do it again.* Well, unless it's a really old, really beautiful piece.

If you're moderately gung ho, skip the stripping and try painting and waxing a junk store find—or give it a coat of Bullseye #3 shellac, which adds a nice aged tone, and wax it afterward. I've even used spray paint and wax. Easier yet, be creative and just add a little trim.

A Charm-Bracelet Table I bought this table for $5. It was very plain. You see tons of them around—I think they're plant stands. The same idea could be used on any table really, but a little round one is especially well suited.

I started with cotton tassel trim and cut it to fit all the way around and, yes, stained it with coffee. Then between each tassel I sewed trinkets from my stash of bits and baubles: a bottle, old keys, glass rings, a bit of a broken necklace, a spool, a glass stopper, a wooden knob—you get the idea. I used quilting thread, which is very sturdy so you use less of it, and a large embroidery needle, which has a larger eye than what's known as a "sharp." For each trinket I just put a couple of stitches in the braid, knotted the thread around the trinket a couple of times, took another stitch or two in the braid, and tied it off. If the objects bang into each other, stagger them so that one hangs lower, the next higher. When you're done, nail the braid around the edge of the table with small black tack nails or brass upholstery tacks.

Papered Furniture One way to "refinish" a piece is to paper it. You can even use pages from an old book, which is what I used on the raw wooden posts of the canopy in my own bedroom. I simply tore out pages from a book, cut them to fit, and glued them onto the posts with O'Glue. After the glue has dried for a day or so, you can give the surface a coat of shellac. Boxes, walls, or whatever can be covered this way, although I don't recommend this finish for a dresser or tabletop that gets a lot of wear.

I went a step further on the bedposts and made book-paper "leaves" for the top—a jokey reference to the carved acanthus leaves that top fancy wooden canopies and columns. A piece of wire taped down the back helps each leaf hold its shape.

"Whaddyacallit" I put together another piece of furniture just for hair accessories—une vanité particulière! My brother found a set of white iron legs on the street, apparently from one of those demilune tables that attach to the wall—the kind you often see at the end of a hallway with a formal flower arrangement on top. Well, this one no longer had its top. I was going to make one, but after finding an ugly jewelry box at a flea market for 25¢, I changed my mind. I covered the box with wallpaper, painted the fronts of the drawers, replaced the

plastic knobs with little loop handles, then glued the box to the legs. Leaning against the wall, with the lid left open, it becomes a peculiarly whimsical piece, doesn't take up much room, and is rather amusing as a functioning object. This piece fits in well with a Victorian theme, but putting something together from disparate pieces is the kind of making-do that fits right in with the Humble look. Whatnot shelves made with wooden spools, sewing boxes made into footstools, fruit-crate creations—if you can't find vintage versions, you may be able to put together your own whaddyacallits!

Collecting

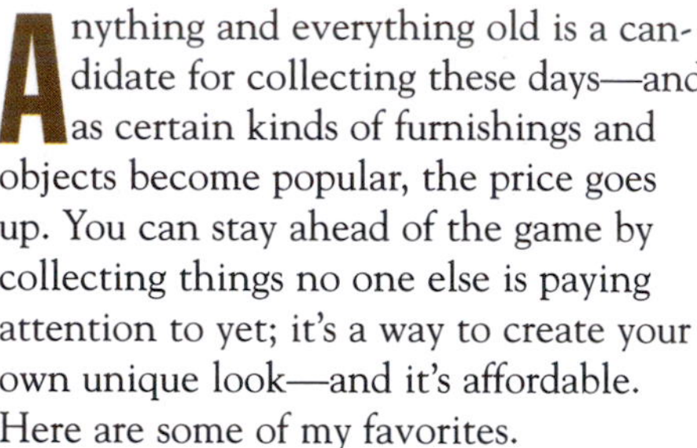

Anything and everything old is a candidate for collecting these days—and as certain kinds of furnishings and objects become popular, the price goes up. You can stay ahead of the game by collecting things no one else is paying attention to yet; it's a way to create your own unique look—and it's affordable. Here are some of my favorites.

Filled containers Boxes or jars filled with small junk—the sorts of things that sit around in someone's garage, workshop, or kitchen drawer for years and years. These are a lot of fun to dig through, and you can get them cheap at auction outlets and junk stores. Separate all the bits into other old boxes and jars, and now you have a healthy supply of sewing needs, small unusual bits of hardware, curtain accessories, buttons, studs, stickpins, small plastic and wooden thingies. They already have a patina, and are great for curtains, embellishing furniture and accessories, or using in collages. If the container and contents are really interesting together, you can display them as is. From time to time I've been lucky enough to stumble upon a box or handbag full of stuff that has nearly fused together with age. I have two doctor's bags filled with old junk that has weathered together for years—visually, they're like pieces of sculpture.

Christmas decorations Beautifully tarnished Christmas balls aren't usually expensive if they're plain, but beware of individually tagged and labeled ornaments or shops and stalls that deal only with Christmas goods—they mark 'em up! Instead, look in thrift shops and junk stores that sell them by the box—and often in a plastic bag mixed in with old garlands and other debris.

Teacups without saucers and saucers without cups These are always good. Just decide on a theme (like pink flowers, gold rims, or all blue) and have fun mixing them together when you get home. You can put together a whole tea set using mismatched but harmonized cups, saucers, lids, and napkins.

The same goes for mismatched silver flatware, candlesticks, pitchers, and trays Set your table with eight or nine old silver candlesticks, all different sizes and patterns and heights. I have a friend who does this. She puts a tall white taper in each for candlelit dinners—much more beautiful and romantic than a stiffly matched pair.

Getting Ahead of the Collecting Game

Forget Hummel and Staffordshire—here's a list of ideas for things to collect now on the cheap—and be envied for later!

Tupperware I'm not kidding. Look for sets that include the *E-Z Cookin* recipe pamphlets, and be sure they have the raised "Tupperware" lettering on them.

Pet rocks, string art, and other oddities from the 1970s.

China figurines depicting 18th-century French aristocrats—you know, the kind wearing powdered wigs that look like statuettes of Louis XIV and Marie Antoinette. Look for tarty-looking men, eyes slightly off center, misapplied glazing. If they're stamped "Occupied Japan" on the bottom, they're probably going to be marked way up—steer clear.

Old hand tools and machine parts These are already becoming collectible—farm implements especially, and to some degree old woodworking tools—but there's a such a wide array of stuff that you're bound to find interesting objects with a sculptural quality that haven't become expensive. Tools made crudely, by hand, are the most beautiful—the humbler the better.

Things that you've no idea what they were for (ask the dealer, who may know) but come in great shapes that you can use as sculpture or turn into a "name that object" party game. If you can't imagine what it is, it may be a real antique. I use some of these in my futuristic hooshes.

Change purses Look for small round-headed rivets in the top fastening—these are really old. The more creased and worn the leather is, the better. Look for purses with odd trinkets and things inside—keys, ticket stubs, pennies, whatever. Part of the fascination of containers is the personality revealed in the contents.

Well-loved and -used books Look for handwriting in the margins, pinned-in notes, crayon scribbles, pencil sketches, old bookmarks, pressed leaves and flowers, and lots of dog-eared pages.

Thermometers Look for all kinds—medical, dairy, candy, meat, and so on. Many of them come in great cylindrical boxes—go for those whenever you find them.

Old scissors These are great hung up as sculpture. The rustier they are, the better. Hang them in rows on the wall, or bunch them together on a wire and hang them en masse.

Old pencils I like the ones that have been used down to the nub and have metal caps with no eraser left. I also like the ones with old company names printed on the sides.

Felt-top hatpins These are something people used to make—cutting the felt into triangles, squares, or circles, padding them, then sewing them by hand onto the head of the pin. The best ones have sequins or tiny beads attached.

Small notebooks or memo books I find small black leather notebooks everywhere. The more writing in them the better—notes, sketches, grocery lists, budgets. Also look for Depression-era tablets: when money was scarce, everything was rationed, including paper. These are the most fanatically filled up, every square inch used, so that each page is a historical work of art. If the whole tablet isn't wonderful, you can excise pages for framing.

Buttons The fancy ones have already become officially "collectible," so look for simple shell buttons with a crusty shell back, gray shell buttons, buttons of wood or metal, doll buttons, shoe buttons, and buttons with a scrap of fabric attached.

Asian statuary carved from soft soapstone I've recently become enamored of these: those pale, beigy-green ornately carved Ming dogs, monkeys, flowers, toothpick holders—and they're cheap at $3 to $15 apiece. Look around for them—you'll find them at all the flea markets. I don't think I can collect anything else, so I hope you'll go for it. A whole little tableful of them would look great.

Button cards and boxes of old buttons are terrific collectibles. They make inexpensive but effective additions to a small composition. And here, in a tiny space, small details have bigger than usual impact.

3·11·7

[Six: **Alienated**]

Pages 94–95
A good-sized statue always adds a spark of life—maybe because it's a facsimile of a human being. This one is a Peruvian statue of Mary Magdalene, made of papier-mâché with real hair. She stands among a collection of columns and pedestals—widely varied examples of the same architectural idea. One is actually a handmade smoke stand topped with a cutting board. Another displays an old hat from the late teens or early twenties that has a plantlike look. The strange branch with white spots that leans behind the statue is the trunk of a Christmas tree; the beige things that look sort of like big fruit slices are foam inserts from film cans. I'm especially fond of the beautifully bound old books stacked by the window; among them is a multivolume Bible from a secondhand store. Between the pages of the Bible were lovely old cards, bookmarks, and other wonderful scraps.

Page 95: The beauty of accidental accumulations.

If you like the inclusive range of Attic, but don't want its degree of clutter, Alienated may be the answer. A collector whose heart is tugged equally by Louis XIV and 1950s modern may find a happy solution in Alienated. It's a great way to put disparate furnishings on speaking terms—as well as to energize an existing scheme that's gotten complacent.

Here are visions that span time, that allow you to view a century of artifacts in one sweep. That's what I aimed for in these rooms. I wanted to create an otherworldly tableau by combining vintage pieces, strange flora and fauna, and humble man-made objects that are modern or futuristic in a naive sort of way with various Gothic embellishments. The idea is to combine unlike things in a calculated fashion—selecting elements for their interest and even shock value, adding them to beloved vintage pieces, and organizing it all so that the pieces relate.

If you're interested in going beyond the romantic, but don't want to relinquish it completely, go alien. Collect stuff no one else would think to collect. Break a few taboos. The best thing about Alienated is that you make it up as you go along.

Among the inspirations for my personal passions I count David Lean's film *Great Expectations*. No matter how many new ideas come along to influence what you're doing at the moment, powerful images from childhood are always certain to appear again and again. My friends say that my bedroom and studio remind them of the seedy, feminine elegance of Miss Havisham's Victorian retreat. Books and movies still stir my imagination and when I set out to venture beyond Miss Havisham's era into something modern, I have *Blade Runner* on my mind. Androids who lurk in rooms filled with fabulous, spooky mannequins and toys with a distinctly Victorian look are my idea of modern. A lot of other relatively recent science fiction has featured archaic-looking machines and gizmos: *Mad Max, Dune, Brazil.* Their effects are born of the 19th-century imaginings of the future—of spaceships and submarines—of a Victorian gentleman named Jules Verne.

Alienated can take in anything. My home harbors a number of cherished vintage collectibles and furnishings. But having been a nonstop hoosher for most of my life,

I like to venture out a bit, and you can too. Go somewhere that excites you. One of my most recent fascinations is plastics. Yes, a major decorating taboo! It all started with a simple piece I discovered at a flea market—a blue butterfly floating in a clear plastic box. This piece mixed all the elements I was looking for: the object itself is humble and homemade; the butterfly is something real from nature; the box is modern mass-produced plastic; and the idea itself is Victorian. The butterfly-in-a-box became a sort of totem for the whole decor, and therefore has a place of honor on the console in the foyer.

Once you add something new to your collections—like clear plastic, in my case—there's so much new stuff to choose from! And plastic is easy to work with since when it's transparent it doesn't overpower. I became fixed on finding clear glass orbs as a "futuristic" element. Spheres of clear glass have a sort of rudimentary-scientific air. I discovered that clear plastic beach balls were inexpensive and easy to find. I also started picking up clear plastic picture frames from secondhand and dollar stores. They'd look horrible mixed together with nice frames—but massed together in a balanced hoosh they are transformed. Clear plastic can turn romantic and Victorian stuff on its head, forcing you to think *now*, not nostalgia. And once you've ventured into the world of plastics, it's easy to get hooked. Plastic leads to the 1970s, and that era supplies another huge category of cheap finds.

But be careful: it's easy for an Alienated scheme to turn into a big junky heap. To guard against that, work with themes. My futuristic concept seemed to call for otherworldly hooshes, so I created some tabletop still lifes that look like weird growths of coral covered with strange underwater plants. They combine mundane, everyday materials (old-fashioned shade pulls, stainless-steel pot scrubbers) with various offbeat collectibles in an energetic jumble that looks as if it's actually growing. Other bits of flora and fauna are all of a piece—among them a strange stuffed bird and a silvery plantlike piece that's even stranger, all displayed under glass domes like specimens of extinct species or plant samples collected on another planet. Glass domes have a wonderfully scientific bell jar look.

Faded, washed-out color is another essential unifying element in Alienated. Except for my chosen accents of blood red and robin's-egg blue, every color in my Alienated scheme is faded. I limited nearly all the newer futuristic elements to faded neutrals and darkened metals.

Collecting old boxes that are already filled or that you fill yourself adds an air

An assemblage of man-made materials can mimic nature: here twigs, seedpods, glass, and clear plastic things are grouped in a knobby construction that includes old wooden shade pulls covered with steel mesh. It looks almost as if all these odd things grew together like a coral reef. An ancient doctor's bag is filled with trotlines, floats, and other bits of crabbing paraphernalia that have weathered together into "found collage." A headboard lamp over the back of a chair adds another eccentric touch and lights up the hoosh at night. A low light placed directly within a hoosh will create an even more Alienated effect.

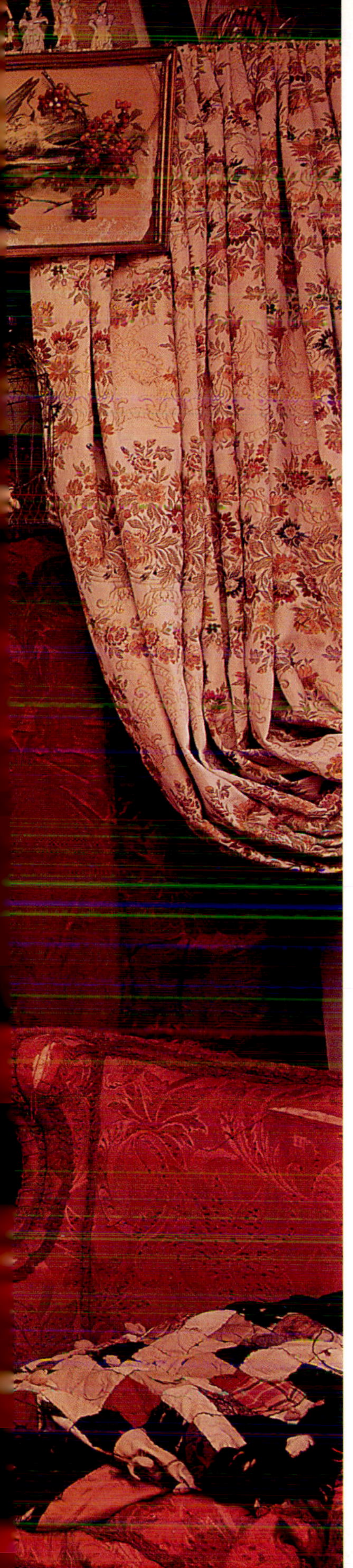

of mystery and excitement to a hoosh—not only in Alienated because there's always something inside to see! Two of my favorite containers are actually old doctor's bags which had been used as catch-alls. One is filled with bits of leather, wood, and string; the other, with crabbing equipment. Both sat open for so many years that bag and contents have melded together into a kind of sculpture.

Plastics, cheap china, old hardware—it's terrific to collect things that are commonplace and show them in new ways. The challenge lies in making a Lucite frame or a 1970s lamp look *appropriate* next to a stack of old books or a Victorian bed. How do you pick the ugliest lamp you can find and incorporate it? By repeating whatever provocative combination you dream up—chrome and Eastlake, fiberglass and gilt, Lucite and lace. Categorization and repetition pull it all together. If room allows, make big statements with furniture or artwork. I'm still looking for one of those 1950s floor-to-ceiling pole lamps—the kind with bullet-shaped plastic lights parading up and down the stem.

Think of it as *future Gothic* and you'll get it immediately.

This dressmaker's dummy wears an Edwardian jacket turned inside out. It's so beautifully constructed it's like sculpture. The jacket and hat display, another small hoosh on a shelf, the curtain hung in the corner, and other bits of drapery all soften the utilitarian look.

Keys to Alienated

Think in terms of creating a landscape. Search out inexpensive oddities to colonize your interior with fantasy flora and fauna. Comb the beach and the woods; nature offers plenty of terrestrial forms with extraterrestrial interest. Cruise junk shops, hardware and dollar stores, and don't forget to survey your own garage. Choose items that appeal to you in some way. If you're tantalized by something ugly, scoop it up. Experiment with tabletop hooshes to see what sorts of combinations communicate with each other—and with your permanent fixtures. If you stay at the dime store level, you can make changes without feeling you've made expensive mistakes.

Calculate your effects. The secret to a successful Alienated scheme is subtle repetition. Choose

A little bit of Victoriana—the deep red carpet and linen and damask-covered sofa—and a scrap of something natural are combined with the shock of plastic in the window treatments in this living room. True Alienated, the room is a mix of periods and elements. Here brocade valances and veils of wrecked silk organza are hung over frosted plastic shower curtain liners with magnets in the bottom. On the coffee table, a collection of glass shades and bulb covers from chandeliers, lanterns, and carriage lamps hold votive candles. One cover is full of bubbles, another is covered with hobnail points—unlit, they look a little like sea urchins. The industrial-looking metal office lamp on the end table is a street find; among candles and warm incandescents, its cool fluorescent glow adds a space-age, Blade Runner *touch.*

whatever outrageous combinations you wish, but divide your decorative furnishings into categories, and repeat each category throughout your scheme. Include a few Victorian or Edwardian objects, elements from nature, clear plastics, and other humble "modern" things.

Add lights in unexpected places. Create subtle special effects by nestling a small light in the middle of a hoosh or at the base of an interesting branch or seashore specimen. Night-lights, tiny halogen desk lamps, battery-powered fixtures, fluorescents, even those hand-held shop lights car mechanics use (the kind with a hook at the top)—any of these can be used to cast Gothic shadows and add an otherworldly glow to your still lifes.

If you can't see it, don't muck with it! A set of curtains can be made simply from panels of fabric hung on rings. You needn't even hem at the bottom because often they're all rucked up and you can't see the unfinished edge. In my bedroom, all most people ever see is the foot of my bed, so that's the part I paid attention to, not the unfinished edge of the curtain around it.

Arm yourself with a roll of thin-gauge black wire. Thin-gauge black wire is one of my secrets—it's inexpensive, extremely easy to handle, and useful for all sorts of things. Use it to put together widgets and gizmos as well as coral-reef assemblages and other fantasy landscapes. Hang sconces and pictures from it—twist and curl the ends of the wire and, if you like, let them show. Use it to attach curtain rings to curtains or curtains to rods—you can push a piece right through fabric like a pin and twist it closed.

Pay particular attention to your palette. If you take anything from this book let it be that the single most important tool to use to bring a room together is *color.* Color can do a lot to draw together a hoosh of disparate objects. Consider a palette of pale neutrals; it's elegant, soothing, and especially pleasing for hooshes that include organic materials.

Make sure there are soft-textured elements in every room. Textiles, upholstery, drapes, and pillows will make a room feel comfortable no matter how bizarre and Alienated your decorative objects are.

Don't forget the barter system. If you like the idea of regular change-ups in your decor, consider swapping or selling unwanted pieces. Like trading baseball cards or comic books, it's easy to trade among friends who have the collecting bug. Take Polaroids of items you want to sell or trade.

Hooshing a Whole Room

Look at your room now: is almost everything pushed up against a wall? The most common mistake people make is to take what's essentially a one-dimensional approach to arranging furniture. We plant the sofa against the longest wall, then back everything else up along the other three walls, creating a tight little ring of furniture broken only by windows and doors. Such stiff symmetry does not welcome life.

Logic and space allowing, let some, if not most, of your pieces "float" in the room (see diagrams on page 106) and the space will feel much more airy and relaxed. This is an elaboration of the concept of *Planes* (see "Spare," page 34). Focus on the whole volume of the room, which includes all that space in the middle of the floor.

How to Arrange a Room

Get up and start pushing furniture around and out of the room. First, remove all your smaller pieces to another room; it's

PAINTED DESERT
PAINTED DESERT

Far left: Raising a bed up high not only gives you a princess-and-the-pea feeling, it allows a serious hoosh at the foot—in this case a couple of chairs, a little table, and pictures hung on the bed frame itself. Custom-carpentered from ordinary lumber, this bed is costumed with linen around the base; the upper posts are papered with the pages from an old book (see how-to on page 91). An antique carved valance of gilded wood across the end gives the effect of a canopy, as do the vintage drapes at the corners—good examples of the way genuinely old elements can add authenticity. The vintage chairs at the foot were missing seat cushions; two large throw pillows turned out to look better than perfectly fitted replacements. Necessity isn't just the mother of invention—it can also be the genesis of style.

Left: The end of a hallway is a made-to-order focal point. The iron candle sconces that line this hall are armatures from an old light fixture hung with thin black wire; they lead the eye to an unusual still life that's pulled slightly away from the wall so that it looks good both from this angle and head-on. Spheres are a repeated element in the scheme: perfect in their simplicity and mysteriously self-contained, they have a lot of appeal. A burst of roundness is a welcome antidote in an environment dominated by straight lines and right angles.

very hard to see clearly when candlesticks, picture frames, books, and so on are lying all over the place. You want to see floor, walls, ceiling, furniture, and nothing else for this step.

Now just start pushing things away from the walls. If you're only able to move your sofa 3 inches out because of space limitations, that's okay. But let everything move toward the center of the room so that the pieces relate to one another. Ask yourself questions like:

- If I'm sitting on the couch, what is in my direct line of vision?

Nails
Egypt
Bath
Stockton
Emmaus
Nazareth
Pemberton

A good example of an Alienated hoosh, this foyer arrangement displays a deliberate repetition of elements—metals and plastics, organic and man-made materials—which is the key to making any unusual mix work. Here two framed works—one blades of grass pressed against felt, one fur pressed against old cardboard—hang on the wall; industrial-looking objects like the rusted metal ball are combined on the tabletop with rock and crystal specimens in cotton-lined plastic boxes. Laced through the arrangement are two rusty lengths of filigree iron wrought with flowers and leaves. They almost look as if they're growing from under the ball. The hanging candelabrum with a doll dress dangling from one arm is a good example of how you can get more impact out of decorative furnishings by letting them float and break a plane in an unexpected way. A dried piece of yucca hovers over the arrangement from a pin while a battery-operated plastic light with a pull chain gives everything an eerie glow.

The tiny tree pictured here was found in the clearance basement of ABC Carpet. The tree, sitting on a chair, gives off a very different impression than if it was sitting on a table. It breaks rules and feels as if it could actually be growing from its soft base—this enhances the mood of strangeness.

- Would I have to move awkwardly or shout to talk to someone in the other chair?
- Is the coffee table against my knees or so far away I have to get up to set my drink on it?
- Do I do beadwork sitting on the sofa but the lamp is by the chair?
- Are the things I need nearby?
- Is the lamp gorgeous but hopelessly dim?

Here's a list of "don't be afraid to do this" things that will help put your furnishings on speaking terms. Don't be afraid to:

- Put a chair in *front* of a wall of shelving.
- Put a table directly behind your sofa.
- Pull your bed into the middle of the floor.

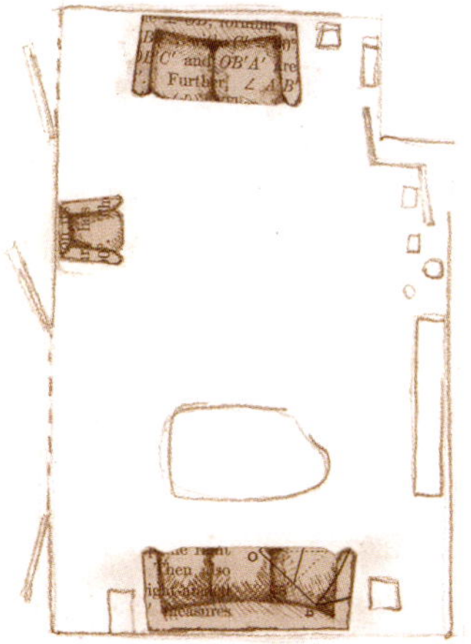

Not floating

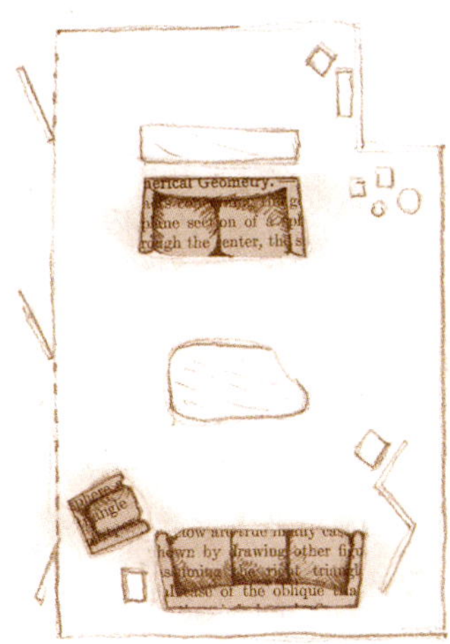

Floating

- Put a chair in front of a large doorway (assuming comfortable passage space).
- Have objects sitting/standing on the floor for no particular reason.
- Use decorative screens.
- Put two same-size pieces of furniture (such as a console and a cupboard) back to back, creating a bay.
- Hang something from the ceiling so that it floats in a corner or above a table (a chandelier, birdcage, art, or large votive, for examples).

In the bedroom, drag that bed out of the corner. Unless you have some quaint cottage in the Alps that has wooden walls or an alcove bed, beds just feel better with at least three sides exposed. Let it be important. A bed is really a grand, sumptuous thing. Don't shove it into the corner.

If all you can squeeze between your bed and the wall is a 1-foot-wide bedside table—that's enough. Put a nice little shaded lamp on it. The light will glow in the corner and be wonderful.

Keep these basic principles in mind when you're hooshing a whole room:

1. The triangle or pyramid principle (see "Attic," page 10). Several dinky pieces of furniture by themselves can look busy and crowded; *adding* a more massive piece to the group, as the apex of the triangle, may actually make a room look less cluttered by visually anchoring and ordering the arrangement. A tall bookcase, an armoire, a big chest, secretary, or hutch can fulfill this function. This is a visual principle—a tall folding screen or a large painting hung on the wall as a backdrop can fill the bill, too. The triangle principle is just as important and useful in arranging large pieces of furniture as it is in a hoosh of small collectibles, and it's essential in an Alienated scheme, where the goal is to get outrageous combinations to look as if they belong together.
2. We also have expectations about the natural order of things—the way elements behave in nature. Do they grow, flow, sink, or float? Consider the nature of an object when you're deciding where to place it. A heavy cement sculpture on a delicate glass table can look dangerously uncomfortable. If it creates the Gothic or otherworldly effect you want, go ahead and subvert these unconscious associations—but be aware of them and calculate your effects.

Comfort Counts A well-hooshed room should be designed first and foremost for comfort. Just as the first requirement for a bedroom is a comfortable bed, the first indispensable piece of furniture for your living room is a big, comfortable couch that you can lie-back-with-a-book on. Virtually everything else in the room can be cunning and inventive. But every room needs at least something soft in texture to make it inviting—a rug, a bed, or curtains can do this, as can pillows and upholstered furniture.

And what about beds? This is where you shouldn't scrimp on yourself. If you're not allergic to feathers per se, treat yourself to real down pillows. And I'm adamant about sheets: if they're not real linen, they must be all cotton.

Think About the Walls

The four walls in a room form an important background or scrim for everything you do in the way of decorating. Palette aside, the actual application of color to your walls is crucial. Personally and professionally, I find walls painted with flat paint uncomfortable and unflattering 99 percent of the time. When color on the wall is broken, even ever so slightly, the whole room changes. Furnishings—antiques in particular—suddenly look as if they belong there; alien objects that shout at each other quiet down. Art is enhanced by the color and texture of the walls, and the room itself will seem to expand. Rooms that have modulated wall surfaces put you at your ease, and you find yourself wanting to stay in them longer.

There are scores of special wall treatments. Most of us have already heard about wall glazing. There are many books on the subject which you can check out. As grand as glazing may be, I actually prefer other techniques. My favorite, and the easiest technique, is the application of a wash. It's simple, cheap, and fast, and doesn't leave the sort of high shine that screams faux finish. A wash can be as dramatic as a browned tobacco stain or as subtle as stark white washed over cream—a finish that's virtually undetectable, but still makes a tremendous difference in the way a room feels. For my own home, I chose a putty wash over off-white and literally just washed the walls with very watered-down paint, rubbing it into the wall with a big sponge.

If you do elect to put a more colorful wash on the wall—green, pink, and so on—I suggest you choose the dullest, drabbest version you can find. Colors that are bright or glow tend to blend poorly for this effect. Try not to get obsessed with finding a very particular hue or shade. There is no such thing as a constant color—the very nature of color is conditional and based on the way light is reflected from a surface. In other words, the color will change when the sun comes in the window directly. It will change in morning light and at sunset. It will look different when an overhead light or a shaded lamp or track light is on, and it will change again when these light sources are combined. More often than not, a color will look deeper and bolder on the wall than it does on a tiny chip, so if you're unsure, go for a softer, more muted version of your color choice.

One last note: cheap paint looks cheap. If you can, spend money on high-quality paint (such as Benjamin Moore or Pratt & Lambert)—especially if you are using a deep color.

Check your local library or bookstore for the dozens of books on paint finishes.

Transforming Space with Stencils

Stenciling is another way to modulate a wall surface and make subtle connections between the borders and planes of an interior space. I stenciled a bit of vine in a few corners of my bedroom, both to repeat the organic element in my overall scheme and to add something a little fancy to the boudoir.

Stencils are actually very easy and fun to do. You absolutely do not have to do the whole room—in fact, I think stenciling over and around every last door and window casing is way overcooked and tacky. But a brief fillip just below the ceiling molding, alongside a door, or here and there above the baseboard can add just the right touch of color and subtle, unexpected drama to a bare corner or patch of wall.

You have lots of options here—there are more patterns to stencil than teddy bears or Swedish designs. There are kits you can buy with interesting patterns. Or if you feel you've got the knack, you can design your own stencil patterns. There are plenty of books around that will show you the way around a wall with a paintbrush, a rag, or whatever weapon you choose for your beautiful attack.

[Seven: ***Alchemy***]

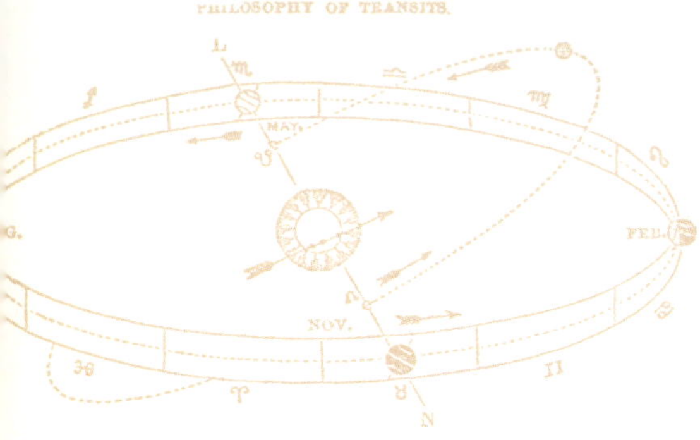

Without looking like a set from a heavy metal video, this opulent space with its rich, deep coloration has a decidedly medieval bent. Just as thick tapestries, drapes, and wall hangings kept out the cold in ancient castles of stone, so is this space cocooned in yards of sumptuous fabric—swathing the walls, framing mirrors, veiling light fixtures. All of it adds up to an interior that's as lofty and baronial as a nobleman's keep—yet Alchemy's spell is woven entirely within the confines of a studio apartment: a single-room-plus-bath, with a tiny nook for a kitchen.

One grand dimension makes a difference—a high ceiling that reaches up to a central skylight. A vintage mantelpiece is another plus, but everything else in Alchemy is the product of sublime costuming, some advanced guerrilla architecture, and the magic of lights and mirrors.

A self-employed painter, Richard Dayne has lived in this apartment for eighteen years, and during that time he's added layer upon layer of comfort. Although he's primarily a painter, Richard also has significant woodworking skills, and he's put them to work creating effective details throughout his home. Hand-carved arches are a repeated motif: in the kitchen, where they form colonnades over the work area; in the bath, where arched niches—"Russian onions," as he calls them—are small but telling focal points. A number of his handmade effects are more complicated and time-consuming than the sorts of DIY projects this book suggests, but the basic principles of display work still apply. Like all the homes in these pages, his scheme runs contrary to a *This Old House* approach. Bob Vila would set out to square it up, clean it up, sand it down—in other words, try to make it look and feel new. Richard's apartment, with its exotic, Moorish-influenced ornamentation, ecclesiastical-looking chairs, and stained-glass lighting, makes you feel serenely comfortable in a setting that could be hundreds of years old.

Like the interior space in Exotic, Richard's decor starts with a rich, deep palette and uses yards of fabric and vintage textiles, but it moves farther back in time for its effects. His carved "Russian onions" are in line with the Eastern and Moorish designs that

Pages 108–109
This is serious cocooning: swathing a room with beautiful old textiles—the velvet coverlet on the daybed, the swags behind the mantel, the table throws—not only looks luxurious but the fabrics absorb and soften sound, turning a potentially noisy city apartment into a private sanctuary. Small spaces like this also benefit from expansive visual tricks: here swags of drapery on either side of a mirror add depth, enhancing the illusion of a window into a looking-glass room beyond. Two tall vases of greenery add fresh spots of natural color—cool counterpoints to the warm palette.

influenced European architecture during the medieval period. And his exotic collectibles, displayed in the living area with his own paintings, are genuine artifacts. Those gathered near the mantelpiece (page 108) include a drum from Tibet, a python skin from Indonesia, and a decorative hookah from Iran—the sorts of things a Marco Polo or a crusading knight might have brought back from his travels.

Richard has also added an alchemical touch of gold to his walls and woodwork, with glazes that contain imported bronzing powders which give the wall surfaces a luminous quality. This interior virtually glows with light—and although the painterly finishes enhance the glow, attention to the quality of the light itself is Richard's real secret. In this one small space, there are no fewer than seventy-eight light bulbs—and not a single one of them exposed. All are veiled or swagged with handmade shades made from scraps of fabric in brilliantly warm colors. It's as if you were surrounded by stained glass: in one corner, a silk shade casts a golden glow on the wall; in another spot, a different shade makes the same wall look rosy. Nothing is bright or glaring. The illumination is hidden, restful, warm, but there is plenty of it.

Glowing color on the walls, multiple light sources, and last but not least—mirrors. It's an old saw that mirrors make a room look brighter and larger, but this apartment proves the point. The mirrors in the bath, kitchen, and living areas are all well-positioned to multiply the sense of space in each area. The tall mirror over the mantel is especially seductive. Swagged with beautiful drapery on either side, it mimics a window into another looking-glass room, even as it doubles the lit candles in front of it. The swags themselves increase the mirror's depth, furthering the illusion of another room beyond this one. In the kitchen area, a mirror is placed, surprisingly, at one end of the counter, where it picks up and doubles the decorative shelving over the sink. Mirrors are a natural in the bath, of course, but here they're extra-large, fancifully framed, and positioned so that they reflect and multiply themselves in long arcades that reach the vanishing point.

As it is in Exotic, the palette here is an unusually rich, deep combination of colors that might feel oppressive in another space this small. But keen attention to illumination—dozens of light sources with exquisitely colored shades, subtly luminous finishes, and multiple light-reflecting mirrors—keeps Alchemy's somber shades looking royally opulent.

Arches—whether Gothic, Romanesque, or Moorish—are a repeated motif here, and most of them are hand-carved. They make their appearance even in the kitchen, where the shelving over the sink boasts graduated tiers that give the effect of a miniature colonnade or cloister walk. Three arches (top shelf) are poised on a row of four (middle shelf) which surmounts a row of five (bottom). Filled with unusual decorative items—vials, boxes, goblets—as well as the usual kitchen paraphernalia, the unit looks like an alchemist's apothecary.

The Best
And Worst

Keys to Alchemy

Look to Europe for inspiration. The ancient villas of Italy, the castles of England, France, and Ireland—many of Europe's famous tourist attractions are potential sources of inspiration. Look for illustrated books on these landmarks as well as general studies of Romanesque, Gothic, and early Renaissance architecture. Closer to home, the Cloisters Museum in New York City has fabulous tapestries and examples of furnishings and architecture from the medieval period. Many U.S. cities harbor Gothic-style churches and cathedrals; visit these if there are examples where you live, and take a look at illustrated books, movies, and dramas that focus on the period (*The King of Ireland's Son*, the *Cadfael* series, and so on). But resist cartoonish heavy metal and sword-and-sorcery effects: you want the castle, not the dungeon.

Pay attention to details—but only those that can be seen. Patient attention to visible details will pay off, but remember the first rule of display: if you can't see it, don't muck with it! Concentrate on color and shape. If you live in a loft with supporting columns, play them up. If your home has doorways or windows with rounded arches, go Romanesque. Accent these elements and repeat their shapes wherever you can. Gothic arches, "Russian onions," Moorish-inspired Spanish architecture, mortared walls and stained glass are all at home in Alchemy; if any of these already exist in your interior, make them part of your theme and build from there. Don't despair if your space is remarkable only in its blandness, however: most of the grand effects pictured here came off a bolt of fabric.

Keep an eye on the ceiling. One of the magical effects of this sort of cocooning is the way it can make a small space feel livably and luxuriously furnished—not crowded. If your ceiling is barely 7 feet up, however, you'll need to accent the vertical to avoid twinges of claustrophobia. An industrial-type loft space with a high ceiling is also a great candidate for the medieval treatment: use lush draperies and hangings to divide the different living areas, cover the floors with old rugs, and

Here a closet has been treated like a giant shadow box of personal memorabilia. The wall surface is completely covered with small photos and drawings, hung salon-style; a cascade of chains, pendants, and bells is hung in front—layers that mimic the simple 3-D effect of a shadow box or diorama.

Like Exotic, incense plays an important role in the atmosphere here, too. Richard has a special silver tray to hold all the paraphernalia of the ritual.

count rough wall surfaces and crumbling plaster as an asset.

Find color cues in antique tapestries and rugs. Russets and earthy red and wine tones from vegetable dyes are prominent in real tapestries and many antique Oriental rugs; their rich, warm colors are especially suitable in a medieval scheme. An especially beautiful rug may be hung on the wall like a tapestry; on the floor, vintage machine-made Orientals with worn spots will fit in just fine.

Try the apothecary look in the kitchen and bath. Use vintage jars, vials, and stoneware crocks for storage, and hang dried herbs over the rafters or above the cupboards—both for their apothecary feeling and for their fragrance.

In furniture, look for bold lines and a masculine, ecclesiastical look rather than looping Victorian curves. The sort of rough, darkened varnish you often find on vintage furniture works fine in a medieval scheme. So do relatively inexpensive turn-of-the-century reproductions of Gothic, Renaissance, and Jacobean styles.

If you're going to fake it, don't fake the cave of Conan the Barbarian. Fake Mont-Saint-Michel!

The Alchemy Potion

Alchemy achieves its special glow from a combination of deep colors and special attention to the effects of light—reflected, refracted, and multiplied.

In the rooms pictured here, a luminous finish has been applied to all the wall surfaces that aren't swathed in fabric. Note the photograph of the sleeping area on page 117: on the ceiling, an undercoat of red oxide was layered over with a transparent emulsion containing gold-toned bronzing powder. The molding was painted a flat, dark green, then glazed with metallic blue-green making it almost iridescent, like a butterfly wing. The imported bronzing powder used here—literally powdered metal—was mixed with banana oil and applied with a brush; two coats were sufficient to modulate the color and give the painted surfaces a subtle sheen.

You may not be able to get your hands on imported bronzing powder, or have the time or patience for such details, but you may want to conduct your own experiments with specialty finishes for walls and trim.

1,200 Paint Effects for the Home Decorator (Ray Bradshaw, North Light Books) is a fun book for paint finishes; its techniques are quick and straight to the point, and it gives you a lot of examples of colors you don't want. But if used as an exaggeration of ideas on color, it can be quite helpful. Also, its wax and paint destressing recipe is what I have always used with excellent results. *Classic Paints and Faux Finishes* (Annie Sloan and Kate Gwynn, Reader's Digest) has good examples and ideas on paint finishes that could work in a decor such as Sir Richard's.

There are so many kinds of paint technique books on the market that I suggest looking for books that show authentic-looking styles (*Paint,* John Sutcliffe, Henry Holt. *Country Finishes,* Judith Miller, Rizzoli, as well as *Classic Paints.* Again, *World of Interiors* is an excellent guide on authenticity, as is *Old House,* Steve Gross and Sue Daley). Your direction should be reality not theatricality; faux finishes are theatrical enough without trying, so choose finishes with an honored past like distemper, vinegar paint, dry washes, waxing, wood graining and tortoiseshell if you're up to it, and subtle dragging. All of these techniques generally have a reality to them, and

Multiple sources and levels of lighting are crucial to keeping this scheme rich rather than somber. Over the bedside table are three lamps at different heights. One of them is hung pendant-style from the ceiling; another is mounted in the corner to the right of the bed; the framed painting is lit by two museum lights instead of one. The bed itself is another grand illusion; this one utilizes old porch columns from a salvage yard. The homemade bedside table is covered by a velvet cape—a bit of vintage clothing that's much more interesting than the ubiquitous round tablecloth. Draped over one end of the table so that its beautiful beadwork shows, it hides utilitarian items stashed underneath.

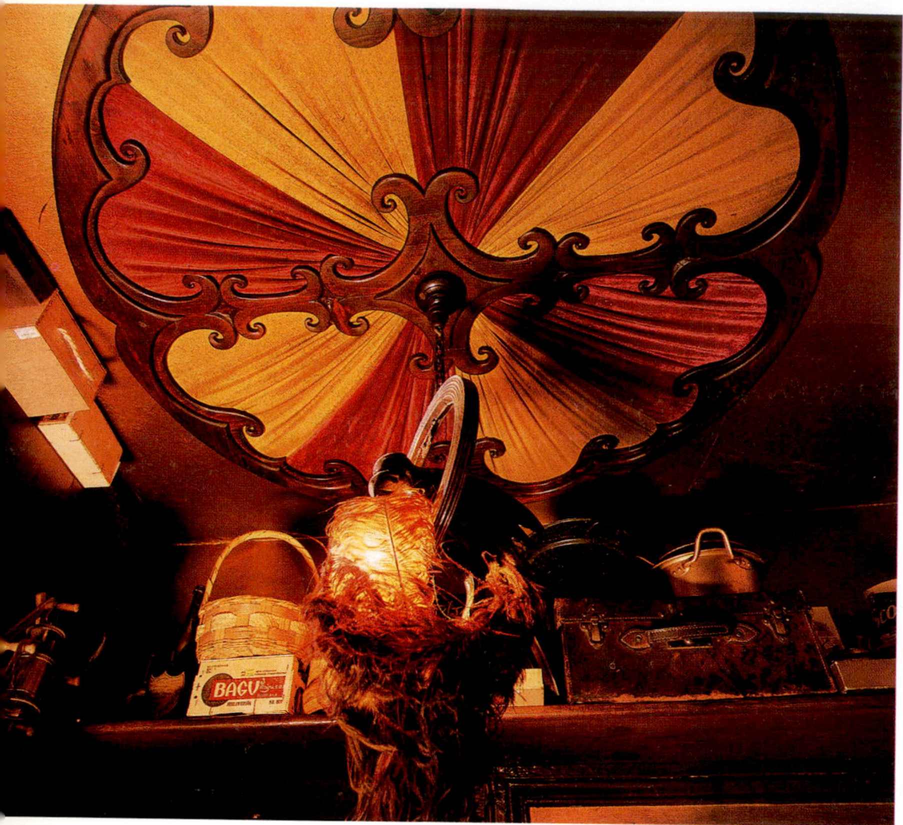

This bold and unusual medallion punctuates the ceiling—a surface most of us ignore. Backed with harlequin silk, it makes a big impact here. A second glance reveals a classic "attic shelf": stashed up high like this, with angled light striking them from below, even humdrum or tattered objects can look seductive—half revealed, half in shadow, mysterious.

therefore are more apt to look good. I strongly advise against sponging and wragging; these effects almost always look homemade and crafty. Glazing, unfortunately, always has that sticky "rubber" sheen that can be unnatural and uncomfortable to me, but I have seen very nice subtle glazes. I prefer oil to water glaze; it doesn't have as bad a sheen, but it is a pain; oil-based products always are.

Lighting

As with using broken or layered colors on your walls, incorporating several levels of light in a room can produce a dramatic change in its ambience. Light is the key to creating the glowing atmosphere of Alchemy, and it's an essential element in any design scheme. Just as draperies and wall art help to connect the planes of an interior and create a harmonious whole, lighting each plane of a room will increase its feeling of comfort and serenity. Multilevel lighting can make a room look larger and warmer, highlighting architectural and decorative details that might otherwise escape notice—and casting romantic shadows where you want the illusion of depth.

Begin with the rooms or areas that are most important to you in terms of comfort. Divide each space into three basic planes—high, middle, and low—and provide lighting at each level. Here are some examples of how each of these planes can be addressed:

- At ceiling height: chandeliers (electric or candled), overhead lights, recessed and track lighting.
- At mid-height: floor lamps, table lamps, museum lights on framed art, wall sconces, standing candelabra.
- At floor level: upright canisters, spotlights, night-lights, votives, hurricanes, table lamps placed on the floor.

Special Placement

You can create especially nice effects with lighting if you break the rules of ordinary placement. Do you have a beautiful old table or chair with claw feet? Place a tiny boudoir lamp on the floor next to it. Try hanging a chandelier in a corner—but at waist height. Put a canister light behind a stand of branches to cast theatrical shadows on the wall. These very simple tricks add drama to any setting.

The Color of Light

The *color* of the light can also work big changes. All of us can attest to the annoying and unflattering light produced by most fluorescent tubes—especially those in department store dressing rooms (you'd think the marketing department would wise up!). We usually laugh, however, at the idea that red bulbs are sexy and pink bulbs are flattering. But in fact, they work! Every one of the bulbs in Alchemy is pale pink, and they produce a soft, flattering glow. Amber lights can also create a cozy effect in rooms with earth-toned palettes.

For quick changes, keep colored silk scarves handy to throw over your lampshades. This is a quick version of what Richard Dayne has done with the lighting in his Alchemy scheme, although his colored silks are cut and stitched to fit. If you're faking it with a scarf, be very careful not to let the fabric get close to the bulb—and like a candle, don't leave it unattended.

The most appealing light of all, of course, is candlelight. Candles are easy, relatively inexpensive ways to divine a mood, and the holders can be some of the odd pieces you've picked up at the flea market—anything from a slender lamp base to hold a taper, to a dessert plate for a fat pillar, to teacups and goblets for votives. Try to find candelabra or holders that incorporate more than one candle—they're especially elegant. If you can find one that's affordable, buy it even if it's tacky. You can always do something to improve the way it looks, and once lit, it's gorgeous no matter what. And try not to limit yourself to tabletops. Standing candlesticks, wall sconces, and suspended candle-fitted chandeliers can transform even the plainest room into a romantic setting.

Special Effects

Like the furnishings in Exotic and most of the schemes in this book, many of the seductive appointments in Alchemy are grand DIY effects. The imposing bed pictured on pages 116–117 is a relatively simple piece of guerrilla architecture, created with salvaged porch columns bolted to an old wooden bed frame. So is the ornate toilet, which is simply a chair placed over the john after removing the seat and replacing it with a hinged lid.

Other features, however, require more time and more skill than the sorts of projects I undertake or suggest in these pages. For those who have the knack and the time, here are a few notes on Richard Dayne's special effects:

Special effect 1: In the kitchen, the facades of carved arches are fastened to the shelves along the front edges; these arches were cut from 1-inch pine and graduate in tiers from three to four to five, giving the effect of a colonnade.

Special effect 2: In the bath (page 122), the small alcoves in the wall were created from identical pointed arches, also carved from 1-inch pine. These were sandwiched together with glue to create forms as deep as the thickness of the walls—which in this case are made of brick and mortar. Enough bricks were chiseled out to fit the forms in; the rough openings around the edges were patched with plaster; and finally all the wall surfaces were covered with linen glued to cardboard backing, then sealed with a waterproof lacquer. The granite birdbath-cum-sink was drilled and fitted by a professional plumber.

Special effect 3: The grand medallion covering the skylight on page 118 is another hand-carved piece. Backed with colorful silk, it gives a beautiful stained-glass effect to daylight. A square skylight cover might be fashioned from molding and precut wood ornaments or filigree from a building supply store like Home Depot.

The Alchemy of Aging

Left and following page: Perhaps the most outrageously exotic space in this apartment, the bath is DIY taken to new heights. The sink is a granite birdbath drilled and fitted with plumbing; the toilet is entirely disguised by an old chair. Discovered on the curb, it was stripped of paint to reveal its wood inlays, and the original chair seat was replaced with a hinged wooden lid. The multiple mirrors create the illusion of long arcades of identical rooms stretching out in two directions. They also multiply the light from four pendant bulbs, each wearing a fringed silk shade cut from an old tuxedo scarf, that hang in each corner. There's even a mirror mounted on the ceiling!

How to Age Metals

Alchemy's emphasis on drapery and great lighting will bring a lot of hardware into play in the form of light fixtures, lamps, drapery hardware, candlesticks, and so on. There's a wealth of possibilities available, and a lot of it in handsome shapes and forms—but you may find yourself running into finishes that are far too bright and shiny for the antiquated look. A polished metal piece with the right sheen can add an opulent touch of silver or gold to your decor, but often inexpensive pieces with a high shine just look tacky. I often find myself needing to tone down the finish on a piece of hardware—and for most of the gently aged looks in this book, it's crucial. Here are some easy ways to do it:

On silver-colored metals: Try pewter black. I always have a bottle of it on hand. You can buy it at a good art supply store, and sometimes full-service paint stores or hardware stores will carry it. It's a type of acid. You either dip small articles into it, or if you've got a larger piece, you brush it on. (It's toxic, so read the directions carefully.) It will work on most metals—wire, nails, screw eyes, thumbtacks, pins—metals that don't have a coating of any sort on them. Take care with aluminum, though—it raises a terrible smell. If the pewter black doesn't seem to work at first, try applying several coats. Sometimes you have to let it stay on the piece an hour or so before it reacts. I pour the leftover liquid back into the jar when I'm done. Never put it down the drain—it will react with your pipes.

If you don't want to mess with pewter black or it just doesn't do the trick on the object, go to plan B: black spray paint. Just spray a section at a time and dab it off immediately with a soft rag (a well-worn bit of T-shirt—nothing linty or fuzzy). Let the paint settle back into cracks and crevices, but dab up the excess on broader areas. If you get it too dark, put nail polish remover on the rag and dab some more. If it's too pale, spray it again and dab *lightly*.

On faux gold or brass: You can try pewter black, but the results are mixed. Black spray

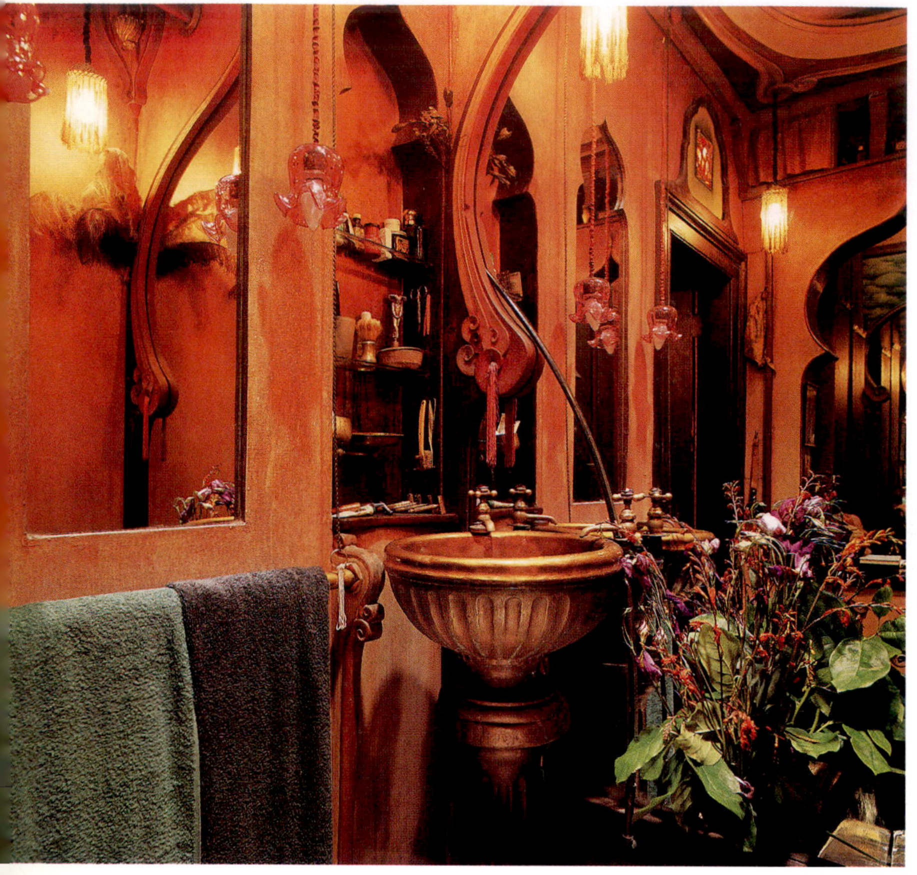

paint will color it, but I prefer brown oil paint: it gives the gold that shows through a nice amber luster. I use Van Dyke brown and brush it on with any brush, then gently wipe it back. This technique works especially well if the surface is textured. If the surface is smooth—and particularly if it's coated brass—you have to dab at it very softly. Let it be dark in cracks and at the edges, and lighter in larger areas. Oil paint is, well, oily, so you have to be careful handling the piece until it's completely dry—wait at least forty-eight hours. And oil paint will never make a completely permanent, stable bond on metal, so I don't recommend this technique if the object is one you're going to handle a lot. I've used it on wall sconces and table

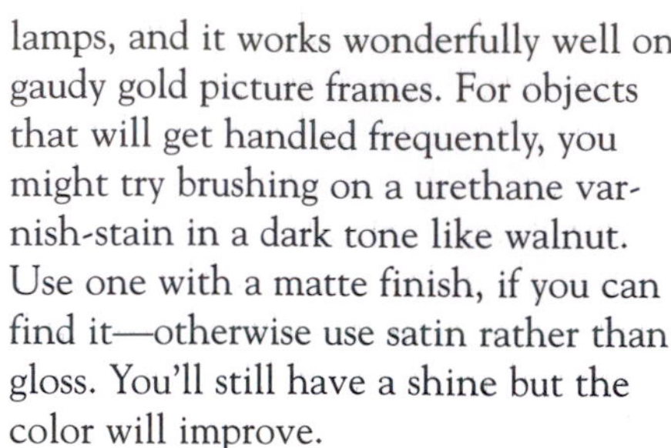

lamps, and it works wonderfully well on gaudy gold picture frames. For objects that will get handled frequently, you might try brushing on a urethane varnish-stain in a dark tone like walnut. Use one with a matte finish, if you can find it—otherwise use satin rather than gloss. You'll still have a shine but the color will improve.

Aging with Heat Last but not least among aging techniques, there's the oven. If you want a permanent tarnish on just about any metal, heat will give you a lovely patina. I've even held small solid metal pieces over a flame with a pair of pliers (be sure you have a trivet or heatproof container to put it in before you go at it).

As for the oven, the temperature setting and how long you leave the piece in there depends: I've left pulleys, small brass ornaments, and candlesticks in a hot oven for twenty minutes and gotten great results. Give it a try on all-metal objects: most likely the worst that will happen is nothing. Need I say you cannot do this with a wired lamp or brass alarm clock or anything else with works that work or parts that could melt or catch fire?

LIGHT FIXTURES

Putting together a good lighting scheme doesn't have to be an expensive proposition. No matter how pricy new lamps in design stores are, you can have your own one-of-a-kind lamps and fixtures without laying out a lot of cash. Just put them together yourself. Ideas for rehabbing old junk store lamps are scattered throughout this book; what follows are step-by-step instructions for three typically fast and inexpensive examples.

CHANDELIER

This is an example of what you can do with a junked chandelier, ball chain from the hardware store, black wire, and some odds and ends from your jewelry box and junk drawer.

I found the brass chandelier with ruined wiring at the junk shop for $3, and used old-fashioned shower curtain rings—the thin metal kind that close like a safety pin—to attach the crystals. Most hardware stores still sell the rings, and you can find the lamp crystals at most flea markets and stores that carry used lamps and fixtures (mine came from a sconce found on the street). I added some old earrings, a string of beads, and flowers from a beat-up old hat; you could also use velvet rosettes, miniature artificial fruits, fancy buttons, tassels, small tarnished Christmas ornaments—whatever pleases you and fits in with your scheme.

Step 1: Start from the finial at the bottom center. Wire the ends of your ball chain and beads to the finial, then swag them out to the crooks of the arms, letting them drape at different levels and allowing the ends to hang.

Step 2: The large end of the shower curtain rings should be about the right size to fit around the bulb sockets; fit them on so that the smaller, clasp ends point directly out, and hang crystals or other ornaments from them.

Step 3: Tie lengths of wire back and forth between the shower curtain rings, stringing on individual beads or ornaments as you go. Here I've twisted every fourth or fifth bead on the wire to make a stopping point so that the beads stay spaced apart at regular intervals. I hung more crystals from some of the wires, as well as from the center point and from the crooks of the arms, making sure all the ornaments hung at varying levels—varied levels is key.

Step 4: To conceal the bulb sockets, I wired old fabric flowers pulled off a hat onto the curtain rings, then sprayed these with coffee and squished them down so none of the petals would get in the way of a low-burning candle. Wetting with coffee—or even plain water—is a good way to make flowers, ribbons, or fabrics stay put—and when they dry they look as if they've been in place for decades.

Don't worry too much about neatness—just twist the wire on and either wrap the ends behind your ornaments, let them stick out, or turn them into viney-looking corkscrews by wrapping them around something slender like a pencil, then pulling the pencil straight out. The main thing is to hang and drape everything at various heights, allowing the chains and beads to make nice deep swags. You can attach chains and ornaments like this to a chandelier that's still wired for bulbs, or pop candles into the sockets of an unwired fixture.

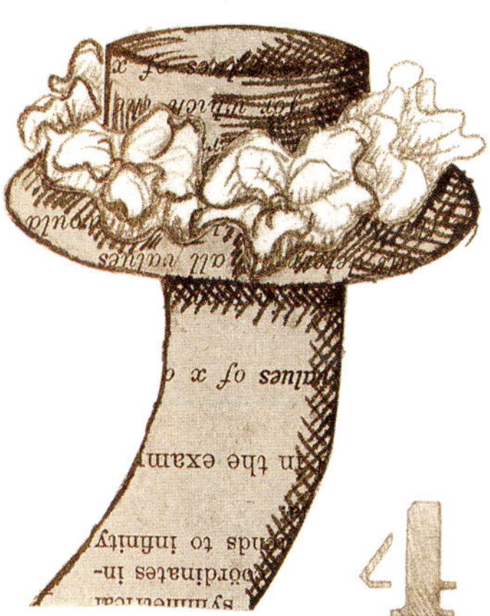

BEADED LAMP

I had a particular lighting problem to solve in my own living room, and this little lamp was the solution. I needed a light over one of my couches, but a standing lamp would have competed with the hoosh I'd put together in the corner, which already consisted of many vertical objects. I decided it had to go on the console table behind the sofa, but there was no room for a table lamp. A clamp-on gooseneck lamp solved the problem.

I loved the functional-industrial look of it, and the price was right—only $12—but a raw bulb would have been too harsh. I'd seen some fabulous glass bulb covers at H, one

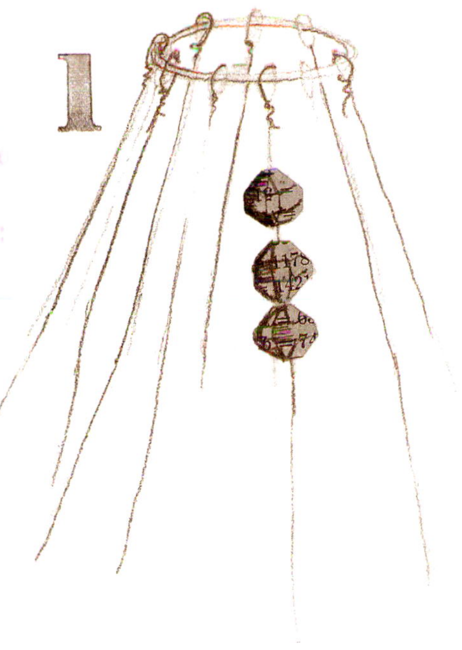

of my favorite shops, but theirs were clear glass, and I wanted a yellow glow. Besides, I had some incredible "vaseline" beads I'd picked up at Beads of Paradise, and they needed a home. The answer was to make my own cover.

BEADED SNOOD

This is a sort of snood made of nothing but beads and wire. You could use any kind of glass beads to make one like it.

Step 1: Make a 1-inch-diameter ring out of medium-gauge wire for a sturdy base to work from. Measure off eight pieces of thin wire, each 2 inches longer than the bulb, and attach them to the ring. You can increase or decrease the number of strands, depending upon the size of your bulb.

Step 2: String each wire with enough beads to curve around the length of the bulb, making a loop at the bottom and twisting the wire until you have enough of a knot to keep the beads from falling off. Count the number of beads it takes on the first wire, then count off the same number for the other seven. Finish and loop the end of each wire before you string the next.

Step 3: Once all eight wires are strung, run another piece of wire about 6 inches long through the bottom loops. Position the top ring on top of the bulb, pull the bottom wire snug around the base of the bulb, and twist it closed.

Snip off most, but not all, of the excess wire—the snood needs to be opened up again when it's time to change the bulb, so leave the ends long enough to twist and untwist them easily.

Spread the beaded wires out until they are evenly spaced.

[Index]

T

U

V